SEX AND THE

*S*PIRITUAL

*L*IFE

"For more than twenty years, our work in marriage restoration has revealed that sex and sexuality is a topic that is frequently suppressed and avoided, and yet our experiences of these things shape our identity. More than ever, we need a book like this in which contributors share their stories and offer hope for others, showing how the good news of the Gospel and the teachings of the Church can give us the tools we need to untwist traumatic experiences of the past in order to learn and heal from them."

Julie and Greg Alexander
Founders of The Alexander House

"Sexuality is a great fire within us and a powerful source of energy but, like an electric line carrying 50,000 volts of energy, it needs to be handled with proper care so that it supplies light and heat without burning the house down. This excellent series of essays honors sexuality for the great and sacred gift that it is. Such an understanding erases the false dichotomy that exists between spirituality and sexuality that sadly is seen most everywhere, both in our churches and within the culture. This is a needed book."

Rev. Ronald Rolheiser, O.M.I.
Author of *The Holy Longing*

"An evangelical friend of mine has a kind of rubric regarding sermons: *I believe it is true; what I want to know is, 'Is it real?'* Patricia Cooney Hathaway has assembled a powerful cohort of Catholic teachers, thinkers, and leaders to present us with the truth of Catholic doctrine on sexuality; and, more importantly, they make it real."

Most Rev. Michael J. Byrnes
Archbishop of Agaña

"In a culture that disfigures the beauty of an authentic Christian anthropology, this book offers an insightful and compelling response and a hopeful pathway toward healthy and holy integration. Patricia Cooney Hathaway and the highly esteemed contributors offer spiritually rich, theologically sound, and pastorally forthright wisdom regarding sexuality, spirituality, and living the Gospel as joyful witnesses of God's unconditional love."

Rev. Msgr. Todd J. Lajiness
Rector and President
Sacred Heart Major Seminary

"*Sex and the Spiritual Life* is a much-needed, mature approach to a subject that is deeply rooted in both theology and the spiritual life. That sex and the spirit are interrelated must never become a forgotten fact or bitter banality. In these pages you will find the lived experiences of those whose approach to sex and the spiritual life has a nobility and freshness that steers clear of naïveté."

Rev. Agustino Torres, C.F.R.
Founder of Corazon Puro

"A rethinking of the mystery and the beauty of human sexuality is important in a changing world and culture, especially for Catholics of every state and walk of life. This book asks real questions and encourages listening to the experience of others. These personal testimonies offer radical hope to Catholics to live what the Church teaches faithfully and joyfully."

Cardinal Joseph Tobin
Archbishop of Newark

"This timely book provides the antidote to the crisis we are living in as a Church and as a society. I enjoyed every chapter and learned from the insights of the contributors who represent the full gamut of sexual vocations. Sharing their stories with humility, vulnerability, and honesty, each writer draws on their personal life experience and the wisdom and healing they have gained through a lifetime of prayer, studying scripture, and connecting to the riches of our Catholic faith. Anyone who desires to live their vocation with integrity and joy should read this book. I highly recommend it."

Bob Schuchts
Founder of the John Paul II Healing Center
Author of *Be Healed*

"This book is the gift we all need to experience renewal and regeneration, both individually and as a parish."

From the foreword by **Fr. John Riccardo**
Executive director of ACTS XXIX

SEX AND THE

*S*PIRITUAL

*L*IFE

Reclaiming Integrity, Wholeness, and Intimacy

Catholic Perspectives
on Married, Single, Ordained, and Religious Life

EDITED BY

PATRICIA COONEY HATHAWAY

Ave Maria Press AVE Notre Dame, Indiana

© 2020 by Ave Maria Press, Inc.

Founded in 1865, Ave Maria Press is a ministry of the United States Province of Holy Cross.

www.avemariapress.com

Paperback: ISBN-13 978-1-59471-991-2

E-book: ISBN-13 978-1-59471-992-9

Cover image © gettyimages.com.

Cover and text design by Katherine Robinson.

Printed and bound in the United States of America.

Library of Congress Cataloging-in-Publication Data
Names: Cooney Hathaway, Patricia, editor.
Title: Sex and the spiritual life : reclaiming integrity, wholeness, and intimacy : Catholic perspectives on married, single, ordained, and religious Life / edited by Patricia Cooney Hathaway.
Description: Notre Dame, Indiana : Ave Maria Press, 2020. | Includes bibliographical references. | Summary: "Sex and the Spiritual Life assures readers of the fulfillment they can experience through "sexual integrity"-a way of life that affirms the presence of God and the sacred in our sexual feelings and expressions. You'll hear from an array of Catholic men and women-married, clergy, religious, and single-whose stories will inspire and equip you to reclaim the joy and wholeness of sexual integrity. In a book that addresses sexuality across a wide range of vocations, challenges, and lived experiences, Dr. Cooney Hathaway and her contributors faithfully present the Church's teachings-and offer practical guidance and inspiration for all who want to experience the freedom and benefits of sexual integrity in their own lives"-- Provided by publisher.
Identifiers: LCCN 2020014054 (print) | LCCN 2020014055 (ebook) | ISBN 9781594719912 (paperback) | ISBN 9781594719929 (ebook)
Subjects: LCSH: Sex--Religious aspects--Catholic Church.
Classification: LCC BX1795.S48 S495 2020 (print) | LCC BX1795.S48 (ebook) | DDC 233/.5--dc23
LC record available at https://lccn.loc.gov/2020014054
LC ebook record available at https://lccn.loc.gov/2020014055

Contents

FOREWORD

SEXUAL INTEGRITY IS
FOR EVERYONE

INTERVIEW WITH FR. JOHN RICCARDO

Man cannot live without love. He remains a being
that is incomprehensible for himself, his life is
senseless, if love is not revealed to him, if he does
not encounter love, if he does not experience it and
make it his own, if he does not participate intimately in it.
—Pope John Paul II, *Redemptor Hominis* (10)

*If you are holding this book in your hands, you are being invited to dis-
cover—perhaps for the first time, or maybe just in a new way—the intrinsic connection between human sexuality and the spiritual life. Through
our bodies, we express the love of God in the world in relationship to other
people. Sadly, when we use our bodies and the bodies of others in ways
that are contrary to God's plan for human love, we can do unimaginable
harm, often in ways that can be very difficult to heal or to talk about.*

*In this interview, Fr. John Riccardo reflects on the vital connection
between human sexuality and authentic spirituality and how that understanding has shaped him both as a man and as a priest.*

Interviewer: Thank you, Fr. John, for agreeing to be interviewed for this book. Where would you like to begin in exploring the relationship between human sexuality and the spiritual life?

I'd like to begin by sharing a part of my personal experience that only in the past few years I have been able to talk about, even with my own siblings: I was sexually abused when I was a child by multiple people, on multiple occasions. Quite frankly, I am still unpacking the devastating impact those experiences had on me; yet I am also grateful that this painful part of my story is being used by God to help bring healing to others who were traumatized in similar ways. I am also thankful that God did not abandon me, even when out of my own hurt and pain I engaged in self-destructive behaviors that also hurt other people.

I think it's safe to say that in our culture today, almost everyone has experienced some kind of trauma related to their sexuality. How can we not, given all we are exposed to every day of our lives? One of the most powerful depictions of this that I've come across is found in the docudrama *The Heart of Man*, written by the author of *The Shack*, William Paul Young. *The Heart of Man* is an imaginative retelling of the parable of the prodigal son and includes testimonies of people whose lives were badly damaged through marital infidelity, addictions to porn or promiscuity, same-sex sexual relationships, or abuse. As *The Wounded Heart* author and psychiatrist Dr. Dan Allender observed in the film, "Sexual abuse is a demonic gift that keeps on giving."

I've rarely come across a truer statement. One of the reasons that so many remain ensnared by this evil is the fact that they are too ashamed to speak of their sexual struggles. It is simply taboo in most social circles to acknowledge them, even to those closest to them. When I listen to the struggles and frustrations of men and women who feel they are somehow stuck in this area of their lives, I am reminded of a passage from Isaiah:

> Can plunder be taken from a warrior,
>   or captives rescued from a tyrant?
>   Thus says the LORD:

> Yes, captives can be taken from a warrior,
>   and plunder rescued from a tyrant;
> Those who oppose you I will oppose,
>   and your sons I will save. (Is 49:24–25)

This passage is such a wondrous foreshadowing of what Jesus came to do for us, to liberate us and rescue us from the tyrant against whom we are powerless. This book is so important because it provides an opportunity to open up the lines of communication, to start a discussion, and to affirm an important truth: shame, especially sexual shame, is not a barrier to God's love. Indeed, when we finally tire of it enough that we are willing to bring the truth of our chains of shame to the light, we find that they become a bridge to personal transformation. And if we are unwilling to step forward and reveal the truth voluntarily, God does not leave us alone in our shame. He has a powerful way of healing us. A line in the movie sums up his healing method: "Shame is . . . an entitlement to do wrong. A lot of us have to get caught. And that is a great and terrifying grace."

Interviewer: This book contains the stories of men and women from all walks of life. Each of them shares their story about what it means to follow Jesus in their state of life as healthy, sexually integrated human beings. What would you want to share with others about what it means to live a healthy, sexually integrated life?

I often tell seminarians in formation, "Being celibate is not the same as being a eunuch." We are not castrated before we take Holy Orders. We are men, with all the drives, desires, and passions other men have. I have grown in the conviction that God created us as men to be generative, to be life-giving. That is one of the dimensions of both physical and spiritual fatherhood.

In *Familiaris Consortio*, St. John Paul II says, "In spite of having renounced physical fecundity, the celibate person becomes spiritually fruitful, the father and mother of many, cooperating in the realization of the family according to God's plan" (16). The flip side of this is that if I don't continually find ways to give of myself, I will *take*. I will use other people. And so, I've learned that I have to keep giving (though not to the point of exhaustion).

As a priest, I don't push my sexuality down or suppress it. I must take all the passion, the drive, and the desire and channel it in life-giving ways. If I don't, I'm in trouble. For example, preaching is remarkably sexual to me, a deep expression of spiritual generation. Preaching isn't merely the transmitting of information or data to another; it is an intimate giving of myself that, hopefully, bears fruit in the life of the other.

I also want to emphasize the utterly important role of healthy spiritual friendships. Twenty years ago, I read somewhere that friendship is like the eighth sacrament.[1] I've never forgotten that, and I've tried to live by the truth of it. The built-in danger of the priestly life is that no one sees me all the time, as in marriage. As a result, I can live with a false sense of myself, since no one is constantly there, filing away the rough edges, so to speak.

For what it's worth, I think priestly formation could greatly benefit from allowing seminarians to live full-time with priests, and do most of their studies online, so they can see firsthand what priestly life is about and so that they can live in a more genuine community, apart from the environment that is, often unintentionally, created in seminaries. We need in our day new models for priestly living, models that look more human than has often been the living situation of priests in the last twenty-five years or so. I need people in my life—people I can trust, who have my best interests at heart, who will come up to me and say, "Hey, what are you doing?" For that, you need true friends.

I can honestly say that apart from the gift of faith, and the sustained habit of daily prayer, the greatest gift God has given me is a number of authentic friendships. I have been abundantly blessed with great friends, both men and women. Unfortunately, not many of these friends are priests. Too many priests seem to lack vulnerability, to be afraid to show who they really are. When a man gets ordained, there can be a temptation to succumb to the massive, unrealistic expectation to be the "answer person" for every member of his parish. We can be afraid to show who we really are—our insecurities and our struggles.

I remember hearing a director of formation years ago say, "The young guys in formation, they look holy, but they're not; the middle-age guys, they don't look holy, and they're not; but the older guys, they don't look holy at all, but they are." These last ones are the priests who have learned to be vulnerable with others. They've learned that you can't walk with someone if you don't understand their struggles. We must be willing to acknowledge together, "I'm broken, and so are you. We don't have to have it all together. We just have to be willing to let God work through us."

Of course, it's important to distinguish between friends and other parishioners who have been entrusted to my care. In every parish, there are people who want to look into a priest's life out of simple curiosity, rather than true friendship. It's essential to set some boundaries. As an example, when someone comes up to me and demands a hug, I've learned to politely say no if I think the person is trying to get past a healthy boundary. Boundaries are also important in counseling or other pastoral settings where a person reveals something very intimate. As a priest and brother, I need to walk with them without revealing in an inappropriate way too much of myself.

That is the difference between pastoral ministry and friendship. No priest can be friends with every member of his parish. So, you have to start with some personal boundaries and then learn over time who can be trusted and has the potential to be a real friend.

Interviewer: What spiritual practices would you recommend for sustaining healthy relationships in one's life?

I think the single most important spiritual practice is sustained, daily prayer. There is no substitute for coming to know, really know, that God created us for friendship with him, and that he calls us friends. And the more I know that I can be transparent with him (since he knows everything anyway), the more I can be transparent with others. At least it's been that way with me.

More than thirty years ago now, someone encouraged me to start the day with a holy hour before the Lord, and it's the single best habit I know. To be sure, in this hour, I have to fight at times the temptation to just fill the time with reading or words. But if I am honest with God there, really bring him the brokenness, unveil the wounds, and listen for his voice and receive his love, then I depart from his presence better able to bring that same love and consolation to the many people I will meet that day.

Has anyone ever told you that God wants to be your friend? To have a relationship with God, you have to be willing to invest time with him, just as you do with any other relationship, both to build up trust and to learn to really listen to what he is saying. One of the people who helped me understand this more than any other was a spiritual director I had in Rome, Fr. David Donovan. He had an art for being really candid. I learned so much from him, even though at first I couldn't stand him! He made me work so hard to learn to express all that was in my head. I would share things with him and ask, "Do you understand?" and he would look at me and simply answer, "No. I don't, John. Help me." That continuous exercise of putting into words all the thoughts I had, all the experiences in prayer that, of course, no one could know if I didn't find a way to share them, was invaluable for me. And it not only taught me how to talk about prayer but it also modeled for me how to listen to another.[2]

Fr. David also taught me that having a relationship with God requires discipline. In *The Four Cardinal Virtues,* Fr. Josef Pieper described the virtue of temperance as "the perfected habit of the ease of the interiorly ordered life."[3] To be frank, my interior life is a mess some days—but I'm not at the whim of emotions because I've been pursuing the habit of temperance. There are lots of ways to do this, such as going to Confession regularly, finding a good spiritual director, and spiritual reading.

Fasting is, at least for me, of great benefit for growing in temperance. Fasting not only helps me to discipline my senses but it also keeps my spiritual senses sharp. Fasting makes me more attentive in prayer, especially in listening to God, and it is a powerful help in interceding for others when I offer up whatever it is I'm fasting from for some other person. It's a little, dinky sacrifice that I make out of love, but for some reason God honors it!

If you're reading this, and you struggle with sexual integrity, I would encourage you to take comfort in the fact that God can use your struggle to help you grow in virtue and, in particular, root out the deadly sin of pride. St. Thomas Aquinas acknowledges this in the *Summa Theologica* when he observes that, in order to help people overcome pride, God allows them to fall into sexual sins—that is, sins of the flesh—that are less grievous, though more shameful, than pride itself:

> From this indeed, the gravity of pride is made manifest. For just as a wise physician, in order to cure a worse disease, allows the patient to contract one that is less dangerous, so that the sin of pride is shown to be more grievous, by the very fact that as a remedy God allows some of them to fall into other sins. (*ST* II, q. 162, ad. 3)

Now, don't misunderstand what I'm saying. Sexual sin is always grave, that is, weighty, because it hinders a person's ability to receive and to give love. And life without love is meaningless. That said, pride is a more serious sin, and, as Aquinas says, God often allows people to fall in one way to cure them of this deeper wound. I remember the first time I came across that quote. I thought, *Wow! Is that ever true!* So, take comfort if you're struggling a bit, and perhaps ask the Lord, "Are you trying to tap me on the shoulder to get my attention about this deeper issue?"

Interviewer: What advice do you give people who come to you with serious issues regarding their sexuality and sexual expression?

The single most helpful thing for me, especially of late, is to offer them what I call a biblical way of seeing reality. Because our culture has pushed God almost entirely out of the picture, after asking a person what they would like from me, I first ask them if I can take a few moments to offer them a biblical way of understanding things. So, maybe they come to me because they're struggling with an addiction to porn, a history of sexual abuse, or homosexual tendencies—it really doesn't matter. They're there, with me, because they're frustrated over their situation, and usually because they feel powerless. They want deep answers. And scripture gives us deep answers.

Ultimately, that answer goes something like this: "The God who created a universe that is 46 billion light years across out of nothing thinks that you are worth fighting for. That's the Gospel. Can I break that open with you a bit more?" No one has ever said to me, "No." In fact, more often than not, those words—You are worth fighting for!—bring them to tears.

There is nothing you can do to earn this kind of love, I tell them. It is not a reward for good behavior. There is nothing you have done, nothing you could ever do, to keep Jesus from fighting for you. "You are, you exist," I share with them, "because God willed you to exist. He brought everything into being out of nothing. And the highlight of everything he made, his Word tells us, is the human race, created in his own image and likeness and destined not only for friendship with him but to be divinized one day.

"But something happened," I tell them. "Clearly, things are messed up in the world that we live in; that's why you're here in my office right now. So, what in the world happened to this creation made by a good God? What happened, scripture tells us, is that one of the creatures God made, who was good, rebelled against God, and he rebelled out of envy of us and the plan God has for us. This creature, the devil, then tricked our first parents at the beginning of our history, and the result of our falling for his trick was that we unknowingly sold ourselves into slavery to him and to powers that we can never defeat on our own: sin, death, and hell. We could say, this is the bad news."

At this point, I ask, "Have you ever done something that you didn't want to do, that you knew you shouldn't do, that you in fact hate doing, but ended up doing it anyway? Me too! Have you ever wondered why? This is the reason. We are impotent against these spiritual powers on our own.

"Ah, but we are not on our own!" I then say. "To rescue us from this situation, God himself became a man, and he did so not to tell stories or to perform miracles, although he did both. He became man to go to war, to free us from the powers of sin and death. 'The Son of God was revealed,' 1 John 3:8 says, 'to destroy the works of the devil.' So, then, you are worth fighting for! And by his death and glorious Resurrection, Jesus has triumphed over this creature and made it possible for you and me to be free again, to live as we were created to live. Would you like that?" (As you can imagine, the answer almost universally here is, "Yes!")

"Well, then, here's all we have to do: the response God is looking for from you and from me is faith. And the easiest way I know to explain faith is this: God's work in me to which I respond. And that response is to surrender to him. What, after all, would be the reasonable response to someone who has rescued you from death, hell, and the devil? Wouldn't it be to trust him? Wouldn't it be to love him with all your heart, mind, soul, and strength?"

This is what I say to those who come to me hurting over various sexual challenges in their lives.

Interviewer: What have you learned from Pope John Paul II's Theology of the Body that has helped you personally and as a minister?

I was blessed to study at the Pontifical John Paul II Institute for Studies on Marriage and the Family in Washington, DC. It allowed me to dive deeply into this pope's work and his other works as well.

I can still remember sitting outside on a bench, reading the Theology of the Body for the first time. As I read about God's original plan for man and woman, I realized that in the beginning, men and women communicated with one another without having to use words, "I'm made for relationship with you, and you for me." There was no fear of being used or objectified by the other before that fateful day when our enemy deceived our first parents.

But then, after the Fall, the glance that was once "naked and without shame" was twisted into something dangerous. Suddenly, the fear of being objectified and used crept into our race, and it has more or less been the history of the relationship between the sexes ever since. As a teacher of mine put it, that history has often frankly been one of "using and conniving in being used." I found in John Paul II's writings a profound, and often challenging, explanation of what I had experienced my whole life as a result of the abuse that happened to me. I appreciated greatly John Paul's teaching in the Theology of the Body because here someone was finally instructing me what the body was for and how to live a thriving human life.

Like many people, when I was young, I heard from various teachers over and over again, "Don't do that. Don't do that! Don't even think about doing that!" But nobody ever told me what *to* do until I read the Theology of the Body. Now, finally, I was getting answers. And they made sense. This not only helped me personally; it filled me with a burning passion to teach what I was learning to others who, I knew, were similarly confused and lost.

I'm so thankful that nothing is wasted on God. It would be easier on my own interior life if I'd never experienced many things that either happened to me or that I chose to do when I was younger. But God uses those experiences now as I minister to others who are still caught up in the struggle. I can speak to where they are, help them to understand and relate to them, and explain it so it makes sense. I've become passionate about putting things in terms of "This behavior is helpful to you" or "This behavior is harmful, and here's why," rather than simply saying, "This behavior is right," or "This behavior is wrong." That didn't help me, I know, because I wanted to know why!

In short, the Theology of the Body helped me to understand and then to teach others to understand that the Gospel is good news for sexuality as well as every other aspect of human living, and that's not something that most people equate with the Church's teaching on these matters.

Interviewer: What are your hopes for this book?

Catholics from every walk of life—single, married, religious, and clergy—are hungry for love and want to experience authentic relationships. As I stated before, one of the reasons why this book is so important is that it provides an opportunity to open up lines of communication, to start a discussion.

Recently there have been a couple of movies about the life of Fred Rogers and his iconic television show. He used to say, "Anything that's human is mentionable, and anything that is mentionable can be more manageable. When we can talk about our feelings, they become less overwhelming, less upsetting, and less scary. The people we trust with that important talk can help us know that we are not alone." I think he was right. Most people I know aren't able to speak out about their sexuality openly; many are too ashamed to acknowledge their sexual struggles.

This book could be just the gift your parish needs to experience renewal and regeneration, both individually and as a parish. Consider reading it in small groups and using it to begin a much-needed dialogue about the connection between human sexuality and spiritual maturity. And as you begin to plant those seeds of hope, I pray that those seeds will bear a rich harvest of souls as those who recognize their own areas of woundedness seek healing so that they, too, can experience the life-changing, liberating power of the Gospel.

INTRODUCTION

PATRICIA COONEY HATHAWAY

When a former student of mine, now a book editor for Ave Maria Press, first approached me about editing a book on sexual integrity, I was intrigued and excited. I have long been concerned that the Church historically has not given people, particularly the laity, a robust approach to sexuality. And now we are all paying a dear price for that across every vocation—broken families, disillusioned parishioners, disgraced clergy, vocations miscarried and abandoned.

When an energy as powerful as our sexual drive is not given constructive outlets or guidelines, other than being viewed as an occasion of sin, it tends to go underground and emerge in ways that are hurtful to us, to others, and to our relationship with God: sexual trafficking and abuse, hookups (sex disconnected from love and relationship), and a wide variety of sexual addictions, including pornography addiction.

Educator and author Parker Palmer tells us that we live in the shadow of our leaders. All of us have been deeply disappointed in witnessing the ripple effect of sin as bishops and priests tried to hide the sexual abuse crisis in the Church, and in doing so violated the souls and destroyed the lives of countless children, adolescents, and adults. But this is not the whole story of our Church. St. John Paul II has provided us with a positive approach to our sexuality through his teaching on the Theology of the Body. Had anyone else written this theology, it would have been critiqued as too good to be true! Since its publication, there have been many other books written on human sexuality as well.

So why another one? What is missing? What is missing is the personal witness and testimony of men and women who have struggled to live by the Church's teaching on sexuality and, in so doing, model for us what sexual integrity looks like. So, I invited Catholic women and men from a variety of vocations and backgrounds to share their personal and professional stories regarding the integration of their sexuality into a healthy spiritual life. My hope is that their wisdom, drawn from personal experience, will enable you, the reader, to gain insight into how to live out your sexuality with authenticity and integrity within a mature, vibrant Christian spirituality.

My Story

Providing some of my own background will help explain why this topic is so important to me. The scriptural passage "I have come so that they may have life and have it to the full" (John 10:10, JB) expresses the goal of my life and my ministry.

This focus began many years ago during my first teaching position as an instructor at Marygrove College in Detroit, Michigan. When students came to talk with me about what was going on in their lives, I realized that there was a disconnect between their Catholic faith and their life experience that could best be summed up in an observation of one young man: "You can't be Catholic and enjoy sex."

To tackle this unfortunate state of affairs, I decided to offer a course titled "Faith and Human Development." Many of these young adults had never considered the possibility that God was inviting them into a personal relationship with him; they had no idea that God was encouraging them to find him in all the circumstances of their lives, including their sexuality. But as we studied Erik Erikson's stages of human development interwoven with James Fowler's stages of faith development, these students came to view their faith as a spiritual journey to wholeness and holiness. I made the decision then and there to devote my professional life to helping people see the connection between their Catholic faith and their human experience as an avenue of God's grace.

I chose Catholic University of America for my doctoral studies for three reasons: First, as a Catholic laywoman in the Church, I wanted a strong background in Catholic theology and spirituality.

Second, I was looking for a consortium of schools that would allow me to pursue the centerpiece of my studies—the relationship between human and spiritual development. Third, Washington, DC, provided me with the opportunity to receive a certificate from the Shalem program in spiritual counseling—and later, a faculty position at the Washington Theological Union, where I taught courses in spirituality and human and spiritual development.

In 1988 I returned to Detroit to marry my wonderful husband and join the faculty of Sacred Heart Major Seminary. It was an extraordinary blessing that enabled me to fulfill my deepest personal desires as a wife and mother and to use my professional training as a theologian in the Catholic Church.

Over the years, as wife, mother, professor, and spiritual director, my commitment to help people grow in wholeness and holiness has only deepened and intensified. I came to realize that many people lacked a clear understanding of their Catholic faith, and most had a false or distorted understanding of the Church's teaching on human sexuality. As one well-educated businessman remarked to me, "I didn't know the Church had anything positive to say about sexuality." And again, as I gave a presentation in which I described sexuality as an avenue of God's grace, a young man in the audience laughingly remarked, "You've got to be kidding me!" Over the years, experiences like these have motivated me to focus special attention on the role of sexuality and its impact on our spiritual lives.

Sexual Integrity and Family Life

After the birth of our son, my husband and I discovered that we were unable to have another child, and so we decided to adopt a child from Russia. At an orphanage outside of Moscow, we adopted a beautiful two-year-old girl. We immediately fell in love with this bright-eyed but scared and very wary little girl. Over time we experienced our daughter's heartache over feelings of abandonment and rejection by her birth parents. We also experienced the consequences of a lack of skin touch—the absence of hugs, kisses, and cuddling that are so essential during the first years of life.

I recalled psychologist Erik Erikson's observation that "the need to experience a confirming face, not only at the beginning of life, but to some extent throughout life . . . is a psychobiological need just as basic as food and water. The infant feels recognized when it senses its very presence has awakened in the parent an inner joy—a joy which is, in return, radiated back to the infant in the parent's countenance, voice and touch."[1]

Throughout the years, with plenty of love, hugs, and kisses, our daughter's deep wound became a scar. The loss would always be there but it did not control her, and she experienced the security that comes from knowing she is deeply loved by her adoptive family and a thoughtful, caring community of relatives and friends. Many adopted children whom we have met have not fared so well. We knew many who, in the teenage years especially, pursued sexual relationships as a way to fill the emptiness they felt inside. But these relationships often exacerbated the situation, causing more hurt, disappointment, and pain.

Our daughter's high school counselor told us that the most vicious fights were often between girls, and always over a boy. With probing, the counselor often found that these girls seldom had fathers who were physically and emotionally present or who gave them a confidence in their femininity such that they did not need to seek it out in unhealthy ways.

These experiences motivated me to speak as often as I could to parents of young and teenage children regarding their own human, sexual, and spiritual development, its impact on their children, and the positive or negative effects of their parenting skills. One new young father told me he had no idea that parenting was such a responsibility; he also had serious misgivings about his capability to nurture the spiritual life of his children when he realized he didn't have much of a spiritual life himself.

Spiritual Direction at Sacred Heart

One of the privileges of my ministry at Sacred Heart Seminary is the opportunity to serve as a spiritual director to people from all walks of life. The purpose of spiritual direction is to accompany individuals who are seeking to grow in their relationship with God. This journey includes recognizing and dealing with anything that blocks growth in that relationship as well as our relationship with others.

Within this context I have had the opportunity to accompany many individuals working through issues of sexuality that they felt were hindering them from growing in love for themselves as well as their love of God. Their stories were both deeply personal and unique: a young man struggling with an addiction to masturbation, a young woman confused about her gender identity, a religious woman involved in a sexual relationship with another woman, a married woman discerning whether to stay in a marriage with a husband consumed with an addiction to pornography, a young woman grieving the end of a marriage, a priest trying to be faithful to his call to priesthood yet discovering the joy of falling in love with a woman. With each situation I have been reminded of the power of sexuality as a force for love, life, and blessing, or as a source of hurt, pain, confusion, and disappointment.

Along with the ministry of spiritual direction, I have also taught a course that enabled students to recognize the crucial difference between their *espoused* theology (what they think they believe) and their *operative* theology (the beliefs out of which they actually live and minister). In her book *Spiritual Direction: Beyond the Beginnings*, Sr. Janet K. Ruffing provides the following example of the difference between the two:

> Thirty-year-old Sister Mary is making her annual retreat. She is seeking greater intimacy with Jesus in her prayer. While on retreat she discovers through the help of her director that although she believes Jesus is loving,

compassionate and interested in her (her *espoused* theology) she actually harbors a hidden fear that drawing closer to Jesus will inevitably result in suffering (her *operative* theology).

Her director suggests that her relationship with Jesus might feel different if she stopped approaching it as if she was going to the dentist. When Mary realizes she is operating out of a theology other than the one she thinks expresses her belief, she becomes free to act on her espoused theology.[2]

Over the years I have recognized the importance of having students identify the negative messages or "scripts" regarding sexuality that many of them have unconsciously internalized from their families, church, and culture. Acknowledging these messages gives the students the freedom to choose and minister out of their espoused theology, that is, the positive, life-giving theology of sexuality they were exposed to through their courses.

Sexuality and the Spiritual Life: Opposing Perspectives

In the many years I have taught the history of Christian spirituality, I have identified two opposing perspectives that have influenced our teaching on sexuality and the spiritual life. One is biblically based, the other based in a kind of spiritual dualism.

The first begins with the Old Testament revelation that God is the author of all creation and that every part of it is good. It continues in the New Testament, which celebrates the Word becoming flesh in human history. Jesus, in the fullness of his humanity, affirms every part of us—body, mind, and spirit—as *good*. The second perspective locates its origin in the heresies of Gnosticism, Neo-Platonism, Manichaeism, and Stoicism. Each promotes a spiritualistic dualism that splits apart things that essentially belong together—spirit against nature, soul against body, reason against passion, *agape* against *eros*, Church against the world. It finds its most influential expression in the teaching of St. Augustine, whose personal struggle with sexual addiction left us with a negative view of sexuality as the chief source of sin.

As Christopher West points out in his book *Theology of the Body Explained*, this negative view of sexuality continues to this day: "A suspicion toward the physical world and discomfort with all things sexual is by no means a neurosis induced by Christianity. It hangs like a dark shadow over all human experience. Yet, the Church still struggles today to counter the spirit good–body bad dichotomy which many people assume to be orthodox Catholic belief."[3]

Within the broader Christian tradition, this spiritualistic dualism often led to an overemphasis on the ascetic life and, in the pursuit of holiness, the decision to leave the world and flee to the desert or monastery to live a life of celibacy as the preferred avenue of God's grace and blessing. And yet, it is important to note that Jesus did not choose to leave the world to find God. He spent his days in the Temple and in the marketplace, teaching and healing, finding God among the people so in need of his message of unconditional love and mercy. He was a man who could enjoy a wedding feast and who was not known for extreme fasting or asceticism; rather, he was a man who deeply needed and loved his friends, and was not afraid to embrace them or touch those in need of healing.

Considering the influence of this spiritualistic dualism within our tradition prompts us to ask the question, What message is communicated about the body when saints such as Catherine of Siena, Francis of Assisi, and Ignatius of Loyola ruined their health in their denial of their bodies' basic needs? What image of God would motivate them to think that God was pleased to have them treat their bodies in destructive ways? Later in their lives, having gained some wisdom, each regretted their earlier decisions, for those choices impacted their ability to minister as effectively as they wished.

In the study of our spiritual tradition, it is edifying to see how God drew each of these saints into a deep relationship with him, but the strange silence around their sexuality is mystifying.

Of course, we presume that these great friends of God must have channeled their sexual drive into their love and service of God and others, but there is no explanation as to *how*. In his book *The Holy Longing: The Search for a Christian Spirituality*, Fr. Ronald Rolheiser states, "Spiritual literature tends to be naïve and in denial about the power of sexuality, as if it could be dismissed as some insignificant factor in the spiritual journey, and as if it could be dismissed at all! It cannot be. It will always make itself felt, consciously or unconsciously."[4]

The Meaning of Sexuality

The word "sex" has a Latin root from the verb *secare*, which means literally to "cut off," "to sever," "to disconnect from the whole."[5] Many people are surprised by the negative connotation, yet does it not express our experience of life? We are pushed out of the warm, nurturing womb of our mothers into a world that will often be experienced, even in the best of circumstances, as arbitrary, inhospitable, or not necessarily committed to our well-being. Feeling incomplete or disconnected, we often search out relationships that will make us feel connected, secure, and whole. And one of the most universal ways of doing this, as the Hogans point out in their chapter, "The Joyful Dance of Sexual Connection," is through our sexuality.

Unfortunately, the term "sexuality," as commonly used today, does not reflect its original meaning. On the contrary, it only carries the very narrow connotation of having sex. For the purposes of this book, we prefer a broader meaning: *Sexuality is our way of being in the world as gendered persons*. It includes our self-understanding as male or female, our body feelings, and our attitudes. Most important, sexuality refers to an all-encompassing energy inside us—the drive for love, community, friendship, family, affection, wholeness, joy, delight, self-transcendence.

This understanding of sexuality is beautifully described by James B. Nelson as "God's ingenious way of calling us into communion with others through our need to reach out and touch and embrace—emotionally, intellectually and physically."[6]

In his later work, *The Intimate Connection: Male Sexuality, Masculine Spirituality*, Nelson further describes sexuality as the desire for intimacy and communion, both emotionally and physically. It is the physiological and psychological grounding of our capacity to love. At its undistorted best, our sexuality is that basic *eros* of our humanness—urging, pulling, luring, driving us out of loneliness into communion, out of stagnation into creativity. Sexuality, thus, is a deep human energy driving us toward bonding and compassion, and without it, life would be cold and metallic. Even in its distorted and destructive expressions, sexuality betrays this fundamental longing. It is God-given for no less than that.[7]

The Relationship between *Eros* and *Agape*

Such an understanding necessitates a renewed interpretation of the relationship between *eros* and *agape*. In his encyclical *Deus Caritas Est* (*God Is Love*), Pope Benedict XVI points out that there are three distinct meanings to love: *eros*, the drive toward communion; *philia*, the love of friendship; and *agape*, self-sacrificing love.[8] Benedict questions the Enlightenment critique that Christianity destroyed *eros*. He admits that the Christianity of the past is often viewed as having been opposed to the body; and it is quite true that tendencies of this sort have always existed. Yet, he maintains that Christianity has not destroyed *eros* but rather has declared war on a warped and destructive view of it—the perspective that *eros* is principally a kind of intoxication, an overpowering of reason that strips *eros* of its dignity and dehumanizes it.

Pope Benedict explains that it is neither spirit alone nor the body alone that loves. On the contrary, it is the whole person, composed of body and soul, who loves:

> Christian faith, at its best, has always considered [the human person] a unity in duality, a reality in which spirit and matter compenetrate and in which each is brought to a new nobility. True, *eros* tends to rise "in ecstasy" toward the Divine, to lead us beyond ourselves; yet for this very

reason it calls for a path of ascent, renunciation, purification and healing. (*DCE*, sec. 5)

The pope insists that only when both dimensions are truly
united does the human person attain full stature. Only thus is
love—*eros*—able to mature and attain its intended grandeur. For
us to be fully human, then, *eros* must mature into *agape*. And in
Jesus, the incarnate love of God, we find the integration of all
three: *eros*, *philia*, and *agape*.

Sexuality and Spirituality: Two Sides of the Same Coin

Given our description of sexuality as the drive for intimacy and
communion physically, emotionally, and spirituality, as well as
a renewed understanding of the relationship between *eros* and
agape, what then, is the relationship between our sexuality and
the spiritual life? Christian spirituality refers to the response we
make to God in Christ through the power and energy of the Holy
Spirit. That response takes place within the concrete experiences of
our lives, which includes our sexuality. Our attitudes toward sexuality can either hinder or facilitate our growth toward a healthy
spiritual life. The very energy that moves us toward communion
with one another is the same energy that moves us into relationship with God.

A Christian spirituality, then, should affirm the presence of
God and the sacred in our sexual feelings and expressions. It
should view sexuality as an avenue of God's grace and see sexuality not as an enemy but as a friend. It is within this framework
that I have invited men and women from every state in life to
share their personal stories and professional insights regarding
their own quest for sexual integrity and spiritual health. My hope
is that their honest description of their struggles and successes will
help others who desire to reclaim this part of their lives in order
to live out their vocations with greater integrity, wholeness, and
intimacy.

About This Book

Because sexuality and spirituality are essential components of the lived human experience, I was careful to seek out the experiences and insights of men and women from every walk of life: married and single (whether by choice or design), those who are ordained or professed members of religious communities, and those whose journey toward sexual and spiritual integrity presents particular challenges, including homosexual attraction and sexual addiction. Finally, I sought the particular expertise of those with considerable experience in forming the next generation of vocations—again, to both marriage and Holy Orders or religious life.

These ten chapters have been organized according to the particular needs of each vocation, beginning with married life (since the vast majority of Catholics marry and have families), followed by the single life (arguably the next largest group), consecrated, and finally ordained. My hope is that these deeply personal perspectives from all walks of life will enable you, the reader, to better understand not only your own vocation, but that of others as well, so that we might learn to better appreciate and encourage one another as we seek wholeness and authentic intimacy. Each chapter concludes with a set of questions that may be used for personal reflection or group discussion.

I am forever grateful to Ave Maria Press for supporting the vision and conviction of my editor, Heidi Hess Saxton, that now was the time to write this book. I am deeply indebted to Heidi for her gifted editorial skills. Each contributor expressed admiration and appreciation for her ability to help them clarify their thinking and refine the quality of their work. I am most thankful to all the staff of Ave Maria Press for the design, layout, and shepherding of this book to publication.

I also want to express my appreciation for the administration and faculty of Sacred Heart Seminary, who have been supportive and encouraging of my efforts to write this book. Lastly, I would like to offer my sincere thanks to the men and women who contributed chapters to this book, for their willingness to be open and vulnerable, and to share their professional and personal experience to help others. At a time when so many Catholics are conflicted about the issue of sexuality and faith, both in how they profess it and in how they live it out, these brave testimonies are a welcome invitation for Catholics from every walk of life to consider where God is calling them to experience healing and growth. Perhaps that is exactly what inspired you to pick up this book in the first place! My prayer for you, then, as you begin to read this book, is that you will find the answers you seek in these pages.

CONTRIBUTORS

In the foreword, **Fr. John Riccardo** reflects upon his experiences as both the former pastor of Our Lady of Good Counsel Parish in Plymouth, Michigan, and executive director of Acts XXIX, a pastoral initiative for priests and parishes whose goal is to create a culture of evangelization and discipleship. Drawing from his experiences as a national speaker, radio personality, and author, Fr. Riccardo explores the intrinsic connection between human sexuality and the spiritual life, insisting that the pursuit of sexual integrity is both a challenge and a grace for *everyone*.

Janet E. Smith, professor emerita of moral theology at Sacred Heart Major Seminary, is a leading authority on issues of bioethics and a renowned speaker on the interrelationship of spirituality and sexuality. She grounds our topic with the first and foundational chapter that addresses the crucial question, "What Is Sexual Integrity?"

Timothy P. O'Malley is director of education at the McGrath Institute for Church Life and academic director for the Notre Dame Center for Liturgy, as well as a husband and father. In chapter 2, "Educating for Sexual Integrity within the Family," O'Malley describes the role of the family in teaching children at every stage of development about the profound connection between sexuality and spiritual life.

The epidemics of sexual addiction and substance addiction as well as the lack of understanding of their causes are the subject of the next chapter, "Sexual Integrity and the Challenge of Addiction." **Jeff Jay** is an addiction counselor and clinical interventionist, as well as a widely published author and speaker. He shares the wealth of his years of experience, including his own journey as an alcoholic toward sobriety and his subsequent ministry to those wounded by sexual addiction. Jay's insights hold out real hope for those willing to walk the path of reconciliation, forgiveness, and conversion.

With their practical spirituality and unflinching honesty, **Timothy Hogan**, a clinical psychologist who specializes in marriage and family life, and his wife, **Karen Hogan**, present a thought-provoking essay titled "The Joyful Dance of Sexual Connection" for chapter 4. In it they share their story of discovering God's Spirit at the core of sexual desire, the inextricable link between sexuality and spirituality for married couples, and key lessons that might help other couples discover the "joyful dance of sexual connection."

In chapter 5, we turn from the married vocation to those who believe God has called them to the single life. We begin with **Susan Muto**, executive director of the Epiphany Academy of Formative Spirituality and a renowned speaker, author, and teacher living her vocation in the world in full-time church ministry. Her chapter, "Sexuality, Spirituality, and the Single Life," reflects upon her own personal journey to sexual integrity as one who chose and embraces the single life.

In chapter 6, "Hidden Treasures for Gay Catholics," **Eve Tushnet**, author of *Gay and Catholic*, describes with a disarming honesty, humor, and deep love for the Catholic tradition her own conversion story. With passion and keen insight, she eloquently expresses the struggle, challenges, and graces of being a member of a community of LGBTQ+ Christians and the "harrowing consequences of the fact that Christ's love and tenderness have become 'hidden treasures' which gay Christians struggle to discover."

Daniel Keating, professor of theology at Sacred Heart Seminary and a member of the Servants of the Word, is the author of chapter 7, "Growing in Sexual Integrity as a Consecrated Man." While acknowledging common elements for all who seek sexual integrity, he speaks with candor and realism about the distinctive components that mark the path toward mature sexual integrity in the lives of celibate men living in a religious community.

Sara Fairbanks, O.P., is associate professor of homiletics at Aquinas Institute of Theology, St. Louis, Missouri, and former vocations director for the Dominican Sisters of Adrian. In her poignant and sensitively written chapter, "Love and Intimacy as a Religious Sister," she explores her personal experience of growth and maturation in her relationship with God, self, and others. She also describes some of the practices she has found helpful in living a healthy, celibate sexuality.

The final two chapters are dedicated to the priestly life. **Bishop John M. Quinn** of the Diocese of Winona–Rochester, Minnesota, contributes a thoughtful perspective on the challenges and opportunities of parish ministry in chapter 9, "Sexual Integrity and the Diocesan Priesthood." Addressing the challenges and graces of seeking sexual integrity in each season of a priest's life, Bishop Quinn speaks of the three essential components of sexual and spiritual integrity for priests, and shows himself to be a true professor, mentor, and spiritual father to numerous priests through their years of ordained ministry.

In the final chapter, "Sexual Integrity in the Formation of Seminarians," Institute for Priestly Formation (Creighton University) theologian **Deacon James Keating** reflects deeply upon his personal experience as a husband, father, and deacon as well as his professional experience as a seminary professor and spiritual director of clerics to offer a perspective on the beauty and purpose of a celibate priesthood. Keating bears witness to the importance of a seminarian basing his priesthood on a personal call from Jesus, and how both priests and married men are signs of the purpose of every human life—to be united intimately with God alone.

CHAPTER 1

WHAT IS SEXUAL INTEGRITY?

JANET E. SMITH

Dr. Janet Smith, former professor of moral theology at Sacred Heart Major Seminary begins by writing the foundational chapter, "What is Sexual Integrity"?

As a former teacher and mentor to seminarians and lay students, Dr. Smith combines the academic with the pastoral as, with great clarity and insight, she presents how John Paul II's understanding of sexual integrity builds upon the tradition of virtue ethics inherited from Aristotle and Thomas Aquinas. She punctuates her presentation with real life stories that starkly bring home the consequences of moral decisions that lead to or away from lives of sexual integrity.

Even young people culturally conditioned to see little connection between sexual intercourse and love (and virtually no valuable connection between sexual intercourse and procreation) can be brought to understand that it is wrong to use another person. In fact, it may be something they innately know.

For instance, one young man I know—presently in his third cohabiting relationship—was recently interviewed about his attitude toward sexual relationships. When asked if he was going to marry the woman with whom he was presently living, he promptly dismissed the idea. "No," he quickly answered, "She is a 'gap-filler.' When I get advanced enough in my career, I will find the woman I want to spend the rest of my life with." Hearing his own words, he ruefully observed, "I sound like a real douchebag, don't I?"

Deep in his being, he possessed the knowledge that persons aren't to be used. St. John Paul II would say that he lacked sexual integrity: this young man was so driven by his passions that he did not allow a concern for the right and good to guide his actions.

Sexual Integrity Defined

The term "sexual integrity" has several possible meanings.

Minimally, it may mean that we tell the truth about our sexual motives and behavior, no matter what that truth is. We could call this "I never told you I loved you" integrity. A person can justify having consensual sex with someone for whom he or she has no respect, and honestly admit even to the sexual partner that the only reason for having sex is the availability of the other person. No responsibilities of any kind are assumed. This kind of integrity is not worthless, but it hardly aligns with the integrity that commands respect.

Another meaning for "sexual integrity" is that we behave reliably in accord with our own set of moral norms. This kind of integrity claims, "There are some things I just won't do." For example, a man may refuse to have sex with anyone under sixteen for fear of exploiting the person (or fear of getting caught!). Again, this kind of integrity is not worthless, but it does not command respect.

St. John Paul II used the term "sexual integrity" to mean that *a person knows the truth about the meaning of sexuality, can abide by that truth, and joyfully acts in accord with that truth.* Such integrity must be based upon respecting the nature of the human person and the realities embedded in the sexual act. We could call this "I will never hurt you and will only do what is good for you" sexual integrity.

John Paul II's understanding of sexual integrity builds on but goes beyond the tradition of virtue ethics inherited from Aristotle (and Aquinas). Aristotle and John Paul II shared the view that in order to act morally a person needs (1) to know what it is to be human, (2) to know which actions are moral, and (3) to have the *freedom* to choose moral behavior and also the *self-mastery* to perform the moral action. They emphasize different elements of moral behavior: Aristotle stressed the central place of *virtue*, or self-control, for moral behavior, whereas John Paul II underscored a *consciousness* of the value of the person and of the need always to respect other persons.

Aristotle and Virtue Ethics

Aristotle can rightly be said to be the father of virtue ethics.[1] He thought that only individuals who possessed virtue would reliably act morally because virtue enabled them to control their passions (or emotions) and thus to be able to choose what is good. A person who possesses virtue has what is known as self-possession. Such individuals can act as an integrated whole; spirit, mind, emotions, and (in this case) sexual attraction work together to enable them to do what is morally good.

Aristotle believed the true challenge for ethical behavior was *having control* over our passions since they can easily move us to prefer what is pleasurable over what is good. The virtuous person is trustworthy and reliable and thus makes good decisions, has many friends, and, in general, is successful and lives well.

For Aristotle, knowing what is good—or the right thing to do—is something most people learn through normal life experience. The experiences of life teach us that lying, stealing, murdering, and committing adultery, for instance, are in conflict with justice (something we naturally know is good). Although many people *know* what *kinds* of action are wrong—such as adultery, stealing, and murder—the real challenge in the moral life is *using that knowledge to govern our behavior* rather than allowing our unruly passions to dictate our actions.

Acquiring correct knowledge of what is right and wrong is not the crucial part of being moral; rather, it is being able to keep the good in sight in the midst of strong passions and to refuse to act in accord with those passions when they would lead to immoral behavior. The virtuous person is also able to *perform* the good action with a degree of ease, and experiences joy even if the choice is difficult and costly. Virtuous individuals are in control of their passions and take *pleasure* in doing the right thing because they are living in accord with their *nature* and their *dignity*.

For Aristotle, gaining the character state of "virtue"—having self-mastery—was not easily done. He thought only a few people could achieve true virtue, which required being born with a good temperament, living in a good culture that had moral education, moral entertainment, and good laws, and finding good mentors to imitate. People could be taught to behave well, but would likely be motivated largely by the fear of punishment and painful consequences rather than by the possession of virtue.

Centuries later, John Paul II built upon the virtue-based ethics of Aristotle. He emphasized the importance of not only knowing which acts are moral but also having what he called "consciousness" of *why* those acts are moral and why acting against them would show a *lack of respect* for self and others. He also spoke much of the need to evaluate one's own interior movements that are a part of sexual attraction—is lust or desire for a feeling of closeness at the root of the attraction, or is there appreciation of the truth of the person behind the attraction?

Consciousness as the Heart of Morality for St. John Paul II

While John Paul II maintained that the virtue of chastity is essential to sexual integrity, he put a stronger emphasis on our need to be conscious of what goods are involved in any moral decision. By "consciousness" he means not just that we know what is moral, but that we are aware of the privilege and responsibility of being a person, free to shape our own character by allowing the truth about reality (rather than selfish desires) to guide our actions. Much of his writing suggests that having a correct view of the value of the human person and of the purpose of sexuality and of the way males and females experience sexual attraction is nearly sufficient to guide us to do what is moral—that is, that such knowledge enables us to control our passions.

At the beginning of his marvelous book *Love and Responsibility*, John Paul II notes that the chief challenge for behaving morally in respect to sexual matters is to transform the self-centeredness of the sexual urge that drives us to desire another for the pleasure that person can provide—that is, to *use* another—to a *love* for the other, that seeks only what is good for the other.[2] Doing so requires a consciousness of certain truths: "Sexual morality results from the fact that persons not only have a consciousness of the finality [purpose] of sexual life, but also a consciousness of being persons. The whole moral problem of using as the opposite of loving is linked to this consciousness."[3] Without the consciousness that those engaging in sex are persons, and that sex leads to the conception of a new person, our sexuality cannot be integrated:

> [In] every situation in which we experience the sexual value of some person, loves demands integration, that is, the incorporation of this value in the value of the person—indeed, its subordination to the value of the person. This is precisely what expresses the fundamental ethical feature of love: it is the affirmation of the person, otherwise it would not be love. If it is saturated with

the proper relation to the value of the person—we have called this relation here "affirmation"—love is fully itself, it is integral love.[4]

Since sex involves persons, John Paul II first establishes what he calls the "personalistic norm": persons are to love and be loved; they are to be affirmed; they are never to be used since they are by nature free and thus meant to be self-determining, to be free to make their own choices.[5]

The basic task here is to develop the concept of love that is just to the person, that is, of love that is always ready to give every man what is rightly due to him on account of his being a person. For what is at times considered "love" in the sexual context can quite easily even be unjust for the person. This happens not because sensuality and affectivity take a particular part in the formation of this love between persons of different sex but rather because partly unknowingly and partly even consciously, an interpretation based on the utilitarian principle is permitted for love in its sexual context.[6]

The Realities of Human Sexuality

Some time ago I spoke with an eighteen-year-old high school student who was defending his decision to have sex with his sixteen-year-old girlfriend. He said that they loved each other and had waited a year in order to get to know each other first.

When I asked him what he would do should she become pregnant, he assured me that that was not going to happen because she was on the pill and he used a condom. I informed him that there are a lot of surprise pregnancies even when precautions are taken; I then asked if he would marry her if she conceived his child. He assured me that abortion was out of the question, yet he admitted that neither of them was in the least bit ready to be a parent.

I then asked him if he wanted his child to be raised by a single mother, if he was ready to pay child support for a child he would not be raising, or if he would be willing to have his child placed for adoption. I asked him if he thought putting his girlfriend in the position where she might have to make these decisions was loving to her. He said he had never thought of these possibilities; they had never discussed them.

He broke up with her soon afterward. I am not certain that my exercise in "consciousness raising" led to that consequence, but I suspect his realization that sex and babies are tightly connected and that babies come with enormous responsibilities had an impact. He might also have realized that he was not acting in a loving fashion to his girlfriend—that they were both using each other for sexual satisfaction more than seeking what was good for the other. They were lacking what John Paul II called sexual integrity. And they were not fully conscious of either the value of the person or of the goods of sexuality.

Both the good of the other person with whom we are seeking sexual intercourse and the good of the child who may be conceived as the result of that intercourse need to be controlling factors in the determination of the moral status of a sexual act as well as our own integrity. All of our sexual choices must be governed by four core truths:

1. We are persons whose dignity is rooted in the ability to know the truth and act in accordance with it;

2. The individual to whom we are attracted is a person who must be respected as a free agent, not an object to be used;

3. All children deserve parents who have made a lifetime commitment to each other so they can experience the love that helps them grow into individuals who know and act in accord with the truth; and

4. The physical experiences and emotional feelings that accompany sexual attraction should be tested to see if they are rooted in a true evaluation of the person to whom we are attracted.

A key way to determine whether we are allowing these truths to govern our choices is to possess "conscious parenthood": We should always be mindful that acts of sexual intercourse with another person can not only produce a child, but make us parents of that child together, and thus we should be prepared for the eventuality. We should want to be a parent only with a person who has or can acquire the virtues necessary to be a good parent, and with whom we can be a good parent.

I became conscious of the responsibilities of sex and babies in a wonderfully natural way, a way that few people today get to experience because family size is often so small. My parents had four children in six years. Because of financial concerns, they practiced what was then known as the "rhythm method" for seven years and then were blessed with a surprise pregnancy, followed by another two years later. I was eleven when the first "surprise" was born.

The presence of a baby in the house immediately transformed me from the neighborhood bratty tomboy into a "little mother" who could not get enough of caring for her little brother (and then eventually her little sister). I think that experience helped me realize the responsibilities that come with sexual relationships. I understood that babies are precious and deserve and need an enormous amount of care from a father and mother who love each other and are committed to each other. I had attained conscious parenthood at a young age. That made achieving chastity quite easy—I was committed to not having sexual intercourse until I met and married a man who would be a good parent.

In John Paul II's view, the simple truth is that because sexual intercourse can lead to the conception of a new human person, people should have sex only with those with whom they are mutually able and willing to be parents. To behave otherwise would be to disregard the need of future persons for loving parental care. It would also be to use the other person as an object to satisfy sexual desires rather than to affirm their goodness and freedom. As John Paul II stated, even if the other person is willing to be so used, use still takes place: "[The acceptance of parenthood] is so important, so decisive that without it we cannot speak about the realization of the personal order in the conjugal intercourse of a man and a woman. . . . For the affirmation of the value of the person may not be separated in both, in a woman and a man, from this state of consciousness and the will 'I can be a mother,' 'I can be a father.'"[7]

Persons should never be used; rather, as the personalistic norm maintains, they should be loved. Affirmation, or the conveying to another that we experience their existence as a good, is an essential element of love. Being willing to be a parent with another is a spectacular form of affirmation, for it means that we are committed to a lifetime relationship with that person. Being willing to be a parent with our sexual partner is a core requirement to ensure that a sexual act is fully affirming and moral. What can be more affirming to another person than to say, "You are the person with whom I want to spend my life and build a family. I believe we are capable of loving each other faithfully over a lifetime and that we will be able to provide children with the love they need."

Asking whether the person to whom you are attracted would be a good parent is an essential litmus test for the suitability of the person as a future spouse. I witnessed a former student of mine come to just such a realization. She, a devout Catholic woman, went off to graduate school and met the man of her dreams, although he was a lapsed Catholic who disdained religion and the Church. Their "chemistry" led her to engage in intercourse with him, but soon they stopped because she realized they were not behaving in accord with God's plan for sexuality. Neither the attraction nor the relationship—a very volatile and passionate one—ended with that realization.

Eventually, I challenged her to either marry or break up with him because she was wasting years of her life if she didn't intend to marry him. She responded that she thought she would never meet a man who fascinated her more, but she didn't want a man so hostile to religion to be the father of her child. I recommended that she write that down twenty-five times and ponder it. Soon she broke off the relationship, and years later she married a man who has been a splendid father to their children and husband to her.

The Raw Material of Love

Love and Responsibility describes additional kinds of self-knowl-edge and knowledge of the other person that should assist a person in making moral choices concerning sexuality. John Paul II referred to what goes on in the interior of a person sexually attracted to another as "subjectivity." He calls the sexual attraction between two individuals the "raw material" of love, and describes various stages through which those attracted to each other must pass to incorporate erotic love—or the love that desires (sexual) union—into *agapic* love, or love that is directed toward the good of the other. John Paul II observes that those who are attracted to each other often squander this raw material, because they do not verify their love in accord with objective truth—the objective value of the human person, the objective meaning of sexual intercourse, the true character of the object of their desire.

The hookup culture very much leads to people squandering the raw material of love. Sexual intercourse is such a casual inter-action these days that many young people have sex with little knowledge of each other. They "hook up" even though they may not know each other's last name. Usually after the consumption of alcohol, they may start "making out," locate a dark room, have sex, and separate the next day without further interaction. Or they may continue to see each other and have sex, and if their stage in life permits it, they move in together, largely to stop paying rent for two places. After cohabiting for a period, they may decide to get married since "the sex is okay, we don't argue that much, and who wants to start all over?" They have never spoken about really serious matters, such as having children and a religious commitment. Their bond is often not strong enough to weather the storms of life.

John Paul II speaks of other ways of squandering the raw material of love. Both men and women tend to idealize the object of their love in a subjective assessment of that person that does not take into account the whole of reality. A male is prone to sen-suality, focusing his interest on a female's sexual values. A female tends toward affectivity, in enjoying the emotions that have been stirred by the attention paid to her. Both male and female tend to idealize the other: "She is so beautiful, she must also be kind, etc." "He carries my heavy packages for me, I feel tremendously cared for; he must be very thoughtful and responsible."

John Paul II speaks of the necessity of the attractions becoming reciprocal and of the need for each person to be tuned in to what the other is feeling. But most importantly, the couple must test their love; they must determine whether their feelings are based on the truth about the other person or whether their feelings—either sexual desire or emotional attachment—have led them to construct a pleasing fantasy.

As they come to know the true character of the other person, should that character be good and worthy of their devotion, they will develop goodwill for the object of attraction. Now they may seek the other as a "good for themselves," but they also seek good for the other in preference to their own good. Alternatively, should they discover that they are not suited to be parents together or to seek a life together, they can terminate the relationship knowing that this investment of time has prevented a lifetime of unhappiness.

When a couple is unwilling to invest in the relationship in this way, the results may be disastrous—not just for them, but for future generations as well. Consider a young woman who got divorced after only a few years of marriage. Many believed the union was doomed to fail for a host of reasons—that she was pregnant with another man's child, that the man she was marrying was himself divorced and the father of two, and that they had moved in together shortly after meeting each other. Before the divorce was even finalized, a "more understanding," "more affirmative" man (recently divorced himself and with a child) entered her life, and they moved in together. Not long after, she came home to find him and some of her possessions gone. They had not fought; he just wanted to be single. She was stunned. She had not tested the love in either relationship— it was mostly sexual attraction, rather than deep commitment to living in accord with truth, that had brought them together.

How to Achieve Chastity

The virtue of chastity is essential for having sexual integrity and for converting the raw material of love into true love. For Aristotle, the work of acquiring sexual integrity was much like an athletic contest—wrestling with the self and receiving either a pleasurable reward (when we have victory over our passions) or enduring a painful punishment (for failing to win the battle). Thus virtue was associated with pleasure and vice with pain.

Many chastity advocates propose techniques for achieving and maintaining chastity, such as not watching porn, practicing "custody of the eyes" (not looking at sexually arousing images or people who are immodest in dress or behavior), and monitoring closely one's consumption of film, music, or reading material that might arouse sexual desire.

John Paul II discusses the value of modesty of dress and behavior, which protects and communicates our sexual values— unlike immodesty, which diminishes personal dignity and too often leads to objectification. The pope speaks of the need for a "pedagogy in love," though he seems to be thinking largely of an education that stresses the need to conduct all love relationships on the basis of the personalistic norm.

John Paul II focuses on the necessity of *understanding* certain truths as a means to sexual morality; those truths are not moral norms per se, but the truths on which the moral norms are based. Again, John Paul II establishes that couples must have respect for the dignity and freedom of each person, and also be conscious that sexual intercourse leads to the conception of a new person who needs the kind of care that only loving, committed spouses can provide. They must also be aware of the movement of their interior life that is leading them to pursue another person, and discern whether they are responding to the truths of the person or allowing their sensual desires or desire for an emotional connection (even fanciful) to guide their choices. Self-knowledge is essential to living the moral life, perhaps especially sexual morality.

Consciousness of the value of each person and of our own interior life should enable us to avoid using another and to learn how to love the other. John Paul II writes, "There is no way to comprehend chastity without the virtue of love. Its task is to liberate love from the attitude to use."[8]

The desire to use comes from selfishness, from thinking it is more important to satisfy one's own desires (sensual or affective) than to respect the other. It is the consciousness of the value of the person that nurtures chastity: "The essence of chastity lies precisely in 'keeping up' with the value of the person in every situation and in 'pulling up' to this value every reaction to the value of the 'body and sex.' This particular effort is interior, spiritual, because the affirmation of the value of the person can only be a fruit of the spirit."[9]

Note here that the knowledge John Paul II thinks is necessary for ethical behavior is not just a simple norm: e.g., "sex outside of marriage is always wrong." What is necessary is a deep understanding of the value of the human person (our own value and that of the person to whom we are attracted) and of the realities embedded in sexual intercourse, and a consciousness of what is drawing us to another person. Ultimately we must test our love by asking such questions as "Am I attracted to the character of this person (in addition to physical attraction), or am I just attracted to physical or emotional feelings I have in response to this person?" and "Is the person to whom I am attracted mature enough to be a parent? Am I mature enough to be a parent? Can our love for each other sustain a lifetime commitment to each other?"

Alarmed by the hookup culture that has become so prevalent on college campuses, some instructors are challenging students to learn how to relate to the opposite sex in a way that allows them to know each other as persons. In the documentary *The Dating Project,* a philosophy professor attempts to help her students rediscover the delights of dating by requiring each of them to invite someone (by phone or in person—no texting!) on a real date. The specifics of the assignment are clearly laid out: the date is to cost ten dollars or less and last no more than an hour.

Initially the students are alarmed by the assignment (they find it easier to have sex than to have a conversation!). But it is very clear that all the participants found the date much more satisfying than their hookups. One young man rejoices that the girl he asked accepted his invitation and says that that experience alone was better than a hookup. Rather than being led by alcohol-fueled desire to approach a woman, he let his attraction to her personhood lead him, which is the proper beginning of a personal relationship.

The Necessity of Grace

For John Paul II, being conscious of the fundamental truths laid out above is essential to achieving chastity. But throughout *Love and Responsibility*, he acknowledges the limitations of that philosophy and indicates that when God is part of the process of achieving chastity, what seems difficult becomes possible if not easy. He speaks of lovers creating their love with the help of God, who will supply the graces necessary. These passages reflect many of the themes of his thought:

> We shall look at love above all as a work of man; we will try to analyze the main ways of his actions in this direction. But the operation of grace is hidden in these actions as a contribution of the invisible Creator, who being love himself has the power to form any love, including love which in its natural development is based on the value of sex and the body, if only people want consciously to co-create it with him. There is no need to be discouraged that this happens sometimes in intricate and convoluted ways. Grace has the power to make straight the ways of human love. . . .
>
> Here it is already evident that the education of love consists of many actions that are interior to the greatest extent, although having their exterior expression, and in

any case are deeply personal. These actions aim at . . .
the integration of love "in" the person and "between"
persons.[10]

Sexual integrity is an essential element of love, an element that
requires habit, consciousness of fundamental values, and reliance
on the grace of God.

Questions for Reflection

1. What is sexual integrity? Why is it wrong to use another
   person?

2. Of what truths must a person be conscious in order to live
   morally?

3. What does John Paul II mean by the "raw material" of love?

4. What does "conscious parenthood" mean, and how does that
   concept govern sexual morality?

CHAPTER 2

EDUCATING FOR SEXUAL INTEGRITY WITHIN THE FAMILY

TIMOTHY P. O'MALLEY

In this chapter, Timothy P. O'Malley, husband, father, theologian, educator, and author of books such as Off the Hook: God, Love, Dating, and Marriage in a Hookup World, *shares his convictions regarding the role of the family in educating for sexual integrity. Such education, he argues, occurs through the modeling of a healthy love relationship between husband and wife, sharing the Church's sexual teaching with adolescents, and preparing young adults to take up a vocation to self-giving love through marriage, single life, or religious life.*

W e expect a good deal from schools. It is the responsibility of the school to form children in the rudiments of mathematics, history, the arts, literature, and the sciences (and within Catholic schools, theology). Students are expected to discover how to relate to peers, to manage their feelings, and to pay attention. At the same time, schools must provide children with extracurricular opportunities, forming students in a variety of skills not covered within the normal school day.

Often, part of this curriculum involves sexual education. This may entail explaining how the male and female sexual systems function. Depending on the school, this instruction may focus in varying ways on both the ethics and practice of sex. Public schools may outline practices of "safe sex" or the ethics of consent within the sexual act. Religious schools emphasize the gift of abstinence, of saving of sex for marriage. Catholic schools will often locate this teaching within an explication of John Paul II's Theology of the Body, pointing young men and women to a responsible use of sexuality as revealed by the divine plan in Genesis and the gospels.

Unfortunately, this high view of a school's vocation is problematic on several fronts. The primary responsibility of sexual education belongs not to the school, but to each child's parents. The school can never be the exclusive space where children learn what it means to be human beings—it is only one of many sources of information and influence that must be taken into account by the *primary* teachers, the parents.

A school may spend several weeks or even an entire semester focusing on an approach to sexual education underlining the integrity of the human person. At the same time, the child is encountering an assortment of media that proposes an alternative vision of human sexuality. The young man is inundated with an understanding of masculinity related to the endless pursuit of sexual partners. The young woman goes to the supermarket and encounters magazines that propose, "Want to be happy? Find the right sexual positions to please your man." Movies, digital media, and popular music profess that anyone who is *not* engaged in sexual activity by a certain age is unlovable, worthless, or ugly.

Increasing numbers of young men and women learn about sex not through school but through the violence of pornography. This toxic, media-driven education in sexuality competes with— and often utterly contradicts—what the schools are teaching. Further, these damaging messages often sneak into the school's curriculum. Much of the language of consent presumes that men and women should have sex before marriage. Education about sexual consent assumes that premarital sex (within the context of committed relationships or random hookups) is a neutral or even positive phenomenon. If everyone agrees that such sex is good, then there's nothing wrong with it.

This view of sex clearly contradicts the Church's teachings on human sexuality, which support the flourishing of men and women alike—within a lifelong marriage commitment. In this lifelong commitment, it is possible for men and women to share in this intimate act as oriented toward their unity as a couple (including the pleasure that is part of sex), as well as to participate in the vocation of parenthood through procreation.

Just as it is the parents (not the school) who are to be their children's first teachers of human sexuality, it is the safe haven of the family that provides the proper space to teach sexual integrity. It is within the family that a child first discovers what it means to be a human being, and it is through the mundaneness of daily life within the home that a child learns about sexual integrity. It is important that families take up this responsibility in a coherent, holistic, and comprehensive manner.

Children are best educated into sexual integrity, first, as it is modeled by their own parents as husband and wife; second, through the concrete proposal of the Church's sexual teaching to the adolescent; and finally, through the support of family members as each child takes up a vocation to married life, single life, or religious life.

Sexual Integrity and the Family

Unlike schools, a family educates children not through a set curriculum but by immersing the child into the life of that family.

This, after all, is how children learn language. Unable to speak at birth, babies gradually become adept at the use of language by imitating their parents and older siblings, through trial and error, and from constant practice within the social context of the family.

The power of familial formation has become evident to me recently, as a dad of young children. In my early days of parenthood, I never really thought about my educational responsibility. I was just trying to survive. I got up in the middle of the night to change the diaper of my son or daughter, fed them when they were hungry, and played a bit with them each evening after getting home from work. As the children developed language, I noticed not only their capacity to repeat word for word what I had just said, but also their imitation of our very styles of speech. Our children were constantly learning from us, often without us even realizing it.

Quickly, my wife and I realized that if we were to educate our children properly, we would need to do so intentionally rather than accidentally. Intentionality is necessary because language is not the only thing that the child learns in the family. The family proposes to the child—from the very moment of birth—a hypothesis about the meaning of life, including sex. The first education toward sexual integrity parents offer a child consists of an *implicit* rather than an *explicit* lesson, modeled through the lived, intimate friendship of married life. By the time the child is ready to hear where babies come from, they have already received formation into sexual integrity through the witness of their parents.

But what if the parents are not themselves formed in this sexual integrity? This isn't—for many young parents today—a hypothetical scenario at all. In my own scholarship and teaching, I have found that many young adults have been formed in a disintegrated vision of sexuality. They have grown up in a hookup culture.

What Is a Hookup Culture?

In my conversations with students, I have learned that a hookup culture cannot be reduced to the act of sex itself. Yes, many young men and women have been taught through digital media that sex is not that big of a deal. They assume that a sexual encounter should be had early in the romantic relationship—no later than the third date. Films have regaled them, proposing a college environment where it's normal—for at least a couple of years—to drink a lot and engage in some ambiguous sexual activity (ranging from sloppy kissing at a bar to sexual intercourse). It's college, after all. They're not ready to settle down.

This vision of human sexuality, if it were only about sex, would be easy to fix. We could counteract this narrative with young people, showing them that sex flourishes only within the context of marriage. We could encourage them to pursue abstinence programs, to recognize that not everyone is either drinking or engaging in ambiguous sexual encounters. We could set a new horizon: "You could be different!"

In fact, this is the approach that many educational institutions—schools and parents alike—have taken. It's also the approach that the Church has taken. We hope that showing men and women the divine plan for sexuality will influence the decision-making of Catholic young men and women. But, ironically, the root problem with the hookup culture is not sex. It is instead a fear of intimacy, an inability to commit to another person.

The hookup depends on an uncommitted ambiguity. Yes, the young person longs for communion with another person. But they're not ready for a serious commitment—the kind of commitment in which one person rearranges his or her life for the sake of another person. There is work or college. There's a sense that love should fulfill the self, leading the person to completion. Until they find a love that "completes" them, the young person seeks occasions of intimacy that brackets out commitment: a drunken make-out here, a random sexual encounter there—what harm could it do?

Of course, those who come to the Church seeking the Sacrament of Marriage have embraced commitment. They're ready to get married. By the time they have children, surely, they're aware of the *necessity* of commitment. They have achieved, perhaps by accident, a degree of sexual integrity. Once upon a time, they hooked up with other people. Once upon a time, they hooked up with one another. But now, they're husband and wife. Sexual integrity will come naturally, right?

This assumption ignores the root cause of the hookup culture: a fear of commitment driven by an assumption that love should be an all-consuming phenomenon. It should complete us, lead us to perfection. However, there are two dangers in presuming that sexual intimacy within marriage is oriented toward this completion of self.

First, if I enter marriage with the assumption that sexual intimacy is about the completion or fulfillment of *myself*, sex will soon become an occasion of conflict within marriage. If I'm not experiencing mind-blowing sex, if I don't have a sexual life that is fulfilling, then perhaps I committed too quickly to this person. Perhaps I should look elsewhere.

Second, this understanding of sexual intimacy reduces my spouse to an object for my personal enjoyment. It is the individual self at the center of the marriage, rather than the communion of the spouses. In its mildest form, I may experience boredom if sexual intimacy with my spouse is no longer an exciting event. I may eventually find myself in a loveless marriage, bored with my spouse and with my life. In its most extreme form, I may determine that this loveless marriage is a sign that I should either leave the marriage or engage in an affair where sex is once again thrilling. I may demand that my spouse fulfill me sexually in ways that harm our relationship. I may turn to pornography, looking for a sexual experience that enables me to escape the pressures and demands of marriage.

Preparing Children for a Future Vocation

If we want to form families that can teach sexual integrity through their very existence, then we'll need to begin with the formation of the couple preceding marriage. In the context of the hookup culture, it's not enough to teach natural family planning and a bit of John Paul II's Theology of the Body. The fundamental cause must be dealt with, the false narrative that sexual intimacy relates to the completion of a self.

In this sense, teaching sexual integrity requires a sexual realism. By sexual realism, we must admit that many of the couples entering marriage formation have participated in the hookup culture. In fact, they may have found their spouse-to-be through a hookup. Likely, they have been effectively catechized through media to see sex as central to love. Their sexual education through this media has focused not on the gift of children, or even the recognition of shared union, but on passionate sexual experiences that facilitate the completion of the self.

Marriage formation can deal with this sexual education in four ways.

First, *it can directly address the hookup culture.* Such conversations are awkward. It's a bad idea to begin with a question like, "How much hooking up did you do?" Instead, a question could be asked early in the process, "Why do you think the hookup is so prevalent among young adults?" Such a question distances the couple from their own experience. They can address their own hooking up without talking about themselves. They may be more open about the problematic dimensions of casual sexual encounters through this indirect question. They may come to recognize the assumptions that led them to hookups, even to see how these assumptions could lead to problems within marriage.

Second, effective marriage preparation *challenges the assumption that marriage—and its related sexual intimacy—is about the completion of the self.* Once again, it's best not to deliver a lecture to the couple. A group of couples should instead be invited to watch a romantic comedy. In this genre of film, the couple always discovers sexual and personal fulfillment with the other. Watching a romantic comedy with a group of couples—some preparing for marriage and others who have been married for years—allows for a fecund conversation about the actual nature of sexual intimacy and friendship in marriage. It also injects a much-needed dash of realism: *Sex isn't everything in marriage. Passion is not the firewood that fuels the flames of nuptial love. Instead, it is commitment to the flourishing of one's spouse through thick and thin.* In this context, sex is an occasion to express real intimacy with the man or woman with whom we share an abiding commitment.

Third, we must also *recognize that there will be couples with significant problems.* Addiction to pornography, for example, is experienced by many men and an increasing number of women. We can't marry these couples and assume that the day-in, day-out quality of nuptial love will automatically heal them. When such problems are revealed, those involved in marriage formation should point the couple to counselors.

Fourth, we need to *attend to the sexual formation of couples even after they're married.* Old habits die hard. If husband and wife have been catechized in a view of sex and romance from a toxic sexual cocktail of hookups, romantic comedies, and pornography, they are going to experience problems. Instead of ignoring these problems, we need couples who can mentor these men and women toward sexual integrity. Such conversations may need to take place not in a group of couples but man to man, woman to woman.

Establish a regular practice of mentorship in marriage preparation. Of course, this mentorship will begin in the period of engagement, but good mentorship will continue in the initial years of marriage as well, as the couple learns (often through the difficulty of lived marriage) that sex is only a small part of marital intimacy.

The Sexual Formation of Children

In a flourishing marriage, one in which the couple is formed in and experiences sexual integrity, children will naturally discover the gift of intimacy. Parents will love one another, expressing this affection through physical signs of hugs and kisses. They won't be constantly gazing at a smartphone. The children will see this love and long to be part of it. In my own marriage, whenever I hug my spouse at the end of a long day, my children run up to engage in a family hug. Intimacy overflows into the life of the family. But there will come a time when it's not enough for the child to learn sexual intimacy *implicitly*. An *explicit* education will need to unfold within the context of the family.

Once more, this education is not reducible to having a conversation about the birds and the bees (although that's a start). It necessitates instead establishing a regular conversation with children in preadolescence relative to sex. Adolescent children quickly become aware that there are competing hypotheses about sexuality. They have learned from a variety of media that there are some who view sex as not that big of a deal. At the same time, their own bodies are awakening to a previously nascent sexual potential. Their friends at school, once just friends, have become objects of sexual desire. They have crushes on one another and begin to hear about sex from others. They often are exposed to "love-crazy" friends, who couldn't imagine living without this boy or this girl.

Yes, there is something awkward about addressing sex directly with our children. The presumption is that no child wants to talk about sex with their parents. And most parents don't really want to talk about sex with their kids. *What if they ask questions that I can't answer? What if they eventually figure out that my own sexual past is, well, a bit complicated?* Yet, study after study has shown that parents—even in the supposed awkwardness of adolescence—remain the most formative figures in their children's lives.

Parents form the religious imaginations of their children. Parents form their children intellectually. Parents are, simply, formative. Therefore, parents must have the kind of explicit conversations about sexual integrity that they may not immediately want to have. Such conversations, though, do not need to be awkward. They can unfold in the following ways.

First, *we should seek out opportunities to talk to our adolescent children.* This is hard! When our children are younger, they tell us everything. They run home from school to declare to us what they did, who they sat next to at lunch, and what they hope to do this weekend. Adolescent children don't always do this. They have developed a hidden or private life that must be respected. But this doesn't mean that conversation ceases. It simply must become more intentional. We must sit down with our children and ask them open-ended (as opposed to yes/no) questions about what is happening in their lives. We need to put down our smartphones and create spaces where our children can talk to us, whether that means special monthly dinner outings or occasional camping trips.

Second, *we must be comfortable with explicit teaching.* Too many parents are afraid of offering a hypothesis to their kids about the meaning of sex. But at a certain stage, they require this hypothesis from their parents. Again, this conversation doesn't need to be a one-time event where we explain the human reproductive system. Rather, it must be a continuous, ongoing exchange. When we are walking with our adolescent children in the grocery store and see a magazine that promises "101 Ways to Please Him in Bed," we should use this occasion to teach our kids. "Do you see how this magazine reduces sexuality to something you employ to gain another's pleasure? God made you for more than that! What are some healthy ways to show love for someone?" There are countless occasions throughout the life of an adolescent to have these conversations. There are movies, music, television, YouTube videos, and conversations from schools that offer an opportunity to form our children for sexual integrity. Eventually, as parents we must also be prepared to present the explicit teachings of the Church—not simply as a list of regulations by which the Church governs our lives, but as a reflection of how God's plan for sexual integrity enriches married life, and how sex within the context of marriage allows for an expression of intimacy and tenderness in which both parties are respected. We can speak about the gift of sex and the accompanying gift of children. This does not have to be taught in a formal setting, turning the home into the classroom. But it must be taught clearly and openly in those moments where it is appropriate to do so.

Third, *parents need to consider the effect of technology on the sexual formation of their children.* No one wants to be the monster who denies their preteen an iPhone or a tablet. But, being a monster in this case is worth it! Adolescents discover too many disordered hypotheses about human sexuality through technological devices. Producers of pornography market to adolescent boys, hoping to hook them on their sites from the time of their youth. Men and women alike discover harmful myths about "normal" masculinity and femininity from Instagram influencers. When technology is misused, it forms men and women in a de-communion, in a non-intimacy that will influence their sexual integrity. They cease talking with one another, unable to maintain eye contact or learn the art of conversation. They expect all communication to unfold through late-night texts. Finding ways to limit our children's experience with technology is an integral part of their formation into sexual integrity.

Lastly, *parents must be prepared to invite mentors into their children's circle of influence.* We must recognize that while we may be the most important figures in our children's lives, adolescents need to have conversations with other adults and their peers. We should cultivate these mentors in the lives of our children to speak to them about the importance of friendship, of choosing the right friends, and about making healthy choices in other areas of life as well. Spend time with other families, so that these experiences of mentorship and friendship may unfold naturally.

Our Children's Vocation and Sexual Integrity

Eventually, our children will leave home. This leaving is hard for every parent. At the same time, it is part of the development of the child. They must eventually choose the form of life that will enable their own flourishing. Our children are gifts to be cherished, not possessions to be controlled. Forming adult relationships with our children isn't easy, but it is important. Even after our children leave home to form families of their own, we continue to have a responsibility as parents to influence and guide them in the formation of their sexual integrity—even as we respect their autonomy as adults.

First, as children begin to date potential partners (or discern religious vocations), *parents have an opportunity to continue forming their children in the gift of fidelity, of the art of mundane love.* Our kids need witnesses of a love that is committed unto the end. Once again, the conversation must be explicit. Adult children may need to hear about the difficulties that the couple underwent in their marriage. Whether the adult child is discerning marriage or religious life, hearing about such difficulties is formative. Life isn't always easy. It's not always fulfilling. Nonetheless, it is through commitment that we really learn to flourish as human beings. Rather than let our kids date entirely on their own, we should *make sure that their boyfriend or girlfriend is always welcome at the dinner table.* We should, in fact, invite them over. Parents can serve as important mentors to a couple, even if one party of that couple is one of their kids.

Second, *parents must serve as an image of both divine and human forgiveness* as our adult children begin to recognize the mistakes that they have made in their journey toward sexual maturity. We must learn to respond not with heavy-handedness ("I told you not to do this!"), but with empathy and understanding. Our effectiveness as parents in the formation of our children comes through the warmth and commitment that we continually offer. Of course, there will be disappointment. There will be sorrow. But it is the responsibility of the parent to offer a possibility of conversion, to restate the hypothesis once more to the adult child that sexual integrity is not about self-fulfillment but about self-giving love.

Third, *we must recognize that our role as mentor to our children continues.* Parents need to be involved in the lives of their children and (God willing) grandchildren. As grandparents, we are given a fresh opportunity to witness to the gift of lifelong fidelity in the midst of the mundane. We may even be able to have conversations with our grandchildren about their own sexual integrity as they enter into adolescence, serving as a mentor to our children's children. Although often tasked with the sexual education of children, schools may in fact be the social entity least prepared to form impressionable minds in sexual integrity.

Because sexual integrity depends upon a total, correct understanding about the nature of human flourishing, the family is ultimately responsible for forming sexual integrity in young men and women. This formation begins with marriage preparation and continues through our potential vocation as grandparents to the next generation of kids.

Questions for Reflection

1. An integrated view of sexuality is taught first within the home, not at school. What in your own background and personal history supports this integrated view of sexuality, both implicitly and explicitly within the family?

2. Hookup culture is not just about promiscuity but also about a fear of intimacy. Where in society do you notice this fear of intimacy?

3. Formation into sexual integrity extends beyond adolescence and continues throughout life. Does your parish or school promote this lifelong formation? If so, how? If not, what might you do to develop this formation?

CHAPTER 3

SEXUAL INTEGRITY AND THE CHALLENGE OF ADDICTION

JEFF JAY

Jeff Jay is a counselor and clinical interventionist in private practice. He is author of Navigating Grace: A Solo Voyage of Survival and Redemption, *and coauthor of* Love First: A Family's Guide to Intervention. *He has worked with numerous individuals and families seeking counseling for themselves and intervention for their loved ones. In this chapter, Jay shares wisdom gained from experience as he describes the problems, challenges, and grace-filled recovery of those suffering from various forms of sexual addiction.*

I have been sober since October 4, 1981. It hasn't been easy; my addiction to alcohol and other drugs nearly killed me, and along the way it distorted other areas of my life, like sex, in ways that caused great damage.

My life started with promise; I grew up in a good home in a good neighborhood and with a good Catholic school education. I had been an altar boy, and I finished high school as president of the student association and a National Merit Scholar. I was also developing a fearsome tolerance to alcohol, drinking vodka by myself. When I went off to the unconstrained world of college, I was a disaster waiting to happen.

It didn't take long. In a few short years, I had dropped out of college, hitchhiked around the country, and fallen deeply into the grip of addiction. Moving from one city to the next, I ignored the concerns of family and friends, sinking lower and lower. At the age of twenty-six, I was penniless and alone, suffering from a bleeding ulcer, a bleeding colon, and transient neuropathy of the legs. Suicide seemed the best option, but I kept those plans to myself.

A family intervention led to a hospital, then a residential treatment center, which led me to the larger community of recovering people. I didn't expect to find so many kind and welcoming souls. They had gone through the same things I had, and they were now sober—and happy. It seemed like a miracle on the order of loaves and fishes, and soon I was in the middle of it.

At the height of my addiction (1973–1981), the sexual revolution was in full flower, and as a young man I was all for it. I had severed all ties with the religion of my youth, and I was proud of my atheism, another intellectual fashion of the times. I wasn't promiscuous, but I was certainly self-centered, and my serial monogamy was indifferent to real commitment. Recovery brought me back to God, but it took years to straighten out the defects of my character.

When I finally returned to the Catholic Church, I was overwhelmed with gratitude; the prodigal son really does have a special sense of appreciation. I started working professionally in the field of addiction treatment in 1986 and have worked with numerous individuals and families as a counselor and interventionist. The challenges and the joys of helping others are deep, especially when I see a person who has the courage to start peeling back the layers of their rationalizations. One thing is certain: sex is a problem for almost everyone.

The Problem of Sex

Managing the sex drive is a challenge for people in every profession, for those who work inside or outside the home, for every level of education, for every race, creed, and color. It's important to acknowledge this because, as the saying goes, "If you don't reveal it, you can't heal it." And if we don't heal it and deal with it, it will deal with us.

Because sex is one of the primary drivers of human behavior—like the drive to attain water, food, shelter, and safety—it cannot be ignored. It is a core function of that tiny and ancient part of our brain called the amygdala, which is part of the limbic system. Our sex drive predates language and is older than civilization.

Sexual intercourse feels good, too. It's pointless not to admit this. For most people, sex feels better than eating and drinking water, though admittedly the latter two are more important. Human beings like pleasure, and we are naturally drawn to pleasurable experiences.

For all these reasons, assimilating sex into our lives in healthy ways is a critical process in human development and an organizing principle of every society. Humans want more than transient sexual gratification; we want real love, connection, and intimacy. We want families and communities. Unbridled sex can destroy all these things. We may veer off from the sexual integrity we desire because of adverse childhood experiences, early exposure to pornography, or traumatic sexual encounters. Whatever the challenge, we are left with the reality of our brokenness, and we can only regain control by facing the issue. Integrating sex into our spirituality is a hallmark of mature faith. It is a challenge and a gift.

An Inside Look at Addiction

Back in the heyday of my addiction, the notion of sexual addiction was all but nonexistent. The governing principle was, "If it feels good, do it." However, as we have come to learn more about addiction, particularly with respect to the brain and human behavior, we have found that the self-centered fear and obsession that lead to drug and alcohol addiction can easily migrate to sex. If a partner is not readily available or we feel abandoned in a relationship, we turn to self-soothing behaviors like masturbation or infidelity. In the evolving world of technology, apps drive the hookup culture, with anonymous sexual encounters easily accessible.

The pleasure associated with masturbation, pornography, and illicit sexual encounters, like drugs, can overwhelm the amygdala and limbic system, and short-circuit our rational judgments. Cascades of dopamine can become addictive, ultimately overwhelming our power of choice. However, resorting to masturbation, pornography, or sexual promiscuity alone does not constitute sex addiction. Addiction has symptoms and phases, and though we may have strong moral, ethical, and religious feelings about aberrant sexual behaviors, a clinical diagnosis is also needed to identify the extent of the problem as well as the most effective treatment.

The Addiction of Pornography

One of the fastest growing problems in the wide world of sex addiction is pornography, in no small part because it is so accessible: Every smartphone, tablet, and computer is a delivery system. Porn drives masturbation and isolation, breaks up relationships, and destroys intimacy. For the purpose of this chapter, we will focus on pornography addiction, though many of the concepts presented are applicable to other forms of sexual addiction.

The first exposure to pornography for boys, sometimes before the age of ten, is no longer a *Playboy* magazine as in previous generations, something relatively tame in comparison to the pornographic videos of the current era. According to Ken Adams, a nationally recognized sex addiction expert, "Porn is no longer just still images. Most people are using technology to view videos, webcams and other immersive technologies. The porn industry is now sophisticated, delivering live action pornography made to order for a customer's desires."[1]

Video pornography on demand produces sexual arousal similar to that of erotic magazines, washing the brain in dopamine, but it also causes a qualitatively different, more extreme, experience. Over time, a kind of tolerance to pornography can develop, necessitating the use of more and more pornography to get the same effect. This mirrors the tolerance developed by a drug addict, who must use more and more drugs to get the same effect. In addition, the user may be driven to more extreme and disturbing forms of pornography, often featuring violence.

Pornography in Intimate Relationships

Some couples wanting to spice up their sex life may think about watching steamy movies together, supposing that a little pornography might recharge their sexual drives. Research has shown, however, that just the opposite is true: The more pornography being used by one or both spouses, the less satisfaction they report in the relationship.[2]

Even for the "casual" porn user, in which an individual's use of pornography has not progressed to the level of addiction, repeated exposure often creates dissatisfaction and depression in the user, both with themselves and in their association with others. Marriages and intimate relationships become arid and dysfunctional, and personal satisfaction with sex plummets. For Catholics, the moral concerns surrounding pornography—a "grave offense" against the human dignity of all concerned—only add to the guilt and shame (see CCC 2354).

Sex is the most intimate physical encounter we can have with another human being. When sex becomes depersonalized, we become depersonalized. We are separated from our innermost selves and our most intimate physical experiences, substituting instead a virtual experience with a screen, which floods our brains with dopamine. As time goes on, more and more exposure is needed to get the same effect.

I've worked with many couples—including Christian couples—who can testify to the devastating effects of porn. Let me tell you about "Anne" and "Bill," who when they came to me had been married for twenty-six years and had successfully raised three great kids. Both had good jobs. They lived in a nice house, were active in their parish, and seemed to have everything going for them in their marriage. No one could see that their marriage was on the brink of collapse. The fact was, however, that Anne and Bill hadn't had regular sex in four years, and had not had any intercourse whatsoever for more than two years.

There was a secret in their household that had destroyed the intimacy they once enjoyed. Anne had no clue what the real problem was, and Bill wasn't telling her. She wanted to be close to him, as they had always been, but he kept pushing her away. He made excuses that he wasn't sexually attracted to her anymore. Of course, this was very hurtful and confusing to Anne. She was a lovely woman, with a brilliant smile and a quick wit. There was no reason to think his excuse was the true reason for the breakdown in their sex life, but Anne wasn't willing to probe further, because his fictional reason was painful and embarrassing to her. They lived separate lives in the same home, living as friends instead of spouses. There were no arguments, just a dull resignation, until Anne finally had had enough.

She made a great effort to restart their sex life, and Bill went along to try to make her happy. He was unable to perform, however, which only deepened Anne's confusion and hurt. Was he really not attracted to her anymore? Was his dysfunction proof?

The truth was that Bill had become addicted to pornography. What had started out as curiosity had gradually morphed into a bad habit, which ultimately became an addiction. It was easy for Bill to become ensnared. Men receive spam emails advertising porn every day, and it is commonplace to click through out of curiosity. Initially, Bill felt the porn was a violation of his value system, but an innocent one. *Whom did it hurt? It wasn't like he was being unfaithful to his wife,* he rationalized. They were in a committed marriage, and he would never dream of cheating on Anne. But pornography . . . that seemed different and somehow safe. It was just a little stress relief, a small, secret pleasure.

But his dalliance with pornography grew as he discovered professionally produced video with airbrushed models and endless variety. He could watch (and virtually "do") whatever he wanted and find release from his sexual urges by masturbating. He watched more, and then he watched more. All modern web browsers have privacy controls that allow anonymous web surfing, so Bill wasn't worried about Anne finding any clues in his browser history. Privacy filtering ensured there would be no evidence.

Over the course of a year or so, Bill became obsessed with his newfound vice. He considered it an innocent form of release, and he could have it anytime he wanted. In the beginning, he and Anne were still intimate, so there were no noticeable issues between them. But gradually he became more and more uninterested in their sex life, and more and more addicted to the tremendous rush of dopamine he experienced by watching infinite varieties of sexual activity. Because their children were away at school or living independently, Bill had ample opportunity to watch porn at home alone. Easy availability combined with frequent opportunity combined with the urge to release more and more dopamine (that is, combined with the craving for more pleasure) accelerated his obsession.

As their sex life evaporated and their cordial daily rituals became unbearable, Anne decided they needed marriage counseling. She was morally and religiously opposed to divorce, but she couldn't envision living this way for the rest of her life. Bill resisted counseling initially and did his best to push it off, but Anne was insistent. She got a personal referral to a respected marriage counselor and made the appointment. She insisted that he come with her and give it a try.

Their first two sessions were only mildly helpful on general matters. Bill played off their lost intimacy and didn't seem willing to address it. They weren't getting to the real issue. The therapist knew from experience there must be secrets in the marriage, so she suggested individual sessions, first with Anne, then with Bill. Anne revealed the depth of her despair and Bill's seeming loss of interest in meaningful intimacy. They were both fit and had no health issues, so she couldn't understand his lack of desire. He was always at home or at work, so there were no signs of an affair, and Anne didn't believe Bill would be unfaithful. She was deeply hurt that he apparently didn't find her attractive anymore, and had seemingly no desire to be close to her.

Bill came to his individual session with the therapist armed with a plan to sidestep the issue of pornography. The therapist had a good idea of what was going on, however. She had already built some rapport with him, so she was able to gain enough trust to do a basic assessment for pornography addiction. Although Bill didn't answer all her questions truthfully, he told her enough to indicate a possible problem. She promptly referred him to a specialist. Bill took the referral when she promised him initial privacy around the issue as long as he took action. She would leave it to him to tell Anne in his own time.

Bill knew he was out of control. He was using porn daily and sometimes multiple times per day, and yet he was getting less and less satisfaction from it. He was watching things that were way outside his value system, and he felt guilty much of the time. He had never been a sexually immoral person, and he knew his obsessive behavior had taken him to a dark place. He had managed to stop for brief periods, but he always went back. He had tried to drastically cut down or change his use of porn, but he always returned to his addictive behavior. Bill began having twice-weekly appointments with a sex addiction therapist who was knowledgeable about pornography addiction.

The therapist started with a thorough assessment, which was a watershed moment in Bill's life. In a sense, it was like a voluntary intervention. Bill came to accept the fact that he was addicted, and that his addiction was breaking up his marriage. He made the decision to pursue treatment with the therapist. He decided to come clean with Anne within three weeks of working with the specialist. Needless to say, Anne was shocked and hurt when she found out about Bill's secret issue. It took time and therapy to rebuild her trust in him and in their relationship. Within three months of beginning the process, however, they tentatively restarted their sex life and wholeheartedly recommitted to their marriage.

Bill continued his intensive sessions with the therapist for six months and discontinued the use of all pornography. He also utilized a local twelve-step group, Sex Addicts Anonymous, which provided him with a spiritual and practical method for regaining control of his life.

Deborah Schiller, MSC, LPC, CSAT, former director of the Gratitude inpatient sexual addiction program at Pine Grove, has found that many people resist the idea of sexual addiction, "Porn addicts rationalize their issue by saying, 'At least I haven't been unfaithful to my wife.' But the wife is thinking: 'He's not present in the relationship. He might as well be with someone else.'"

The good news for the addicted individual, however, is that there is tremendous hope. Schiller has a message for people struggling with pornography addiction: "There is help out there. You can't fix it by yourself, because your brain is giving you error messages. But there are recovery meetings and there are people who are trained to help you. Your prefrontal cortex is offline, and your limbic brain is taking over. You need to borrow someone else's brain to start getting better."[3] Here Schiller is pointing toward the help to be found in twelve-step groups, which will be discussed later.

Some people find it difficult to believe that the use of pornography can rise to the level of an addiction. They think it is quite obviously a moral deficiency, a failure of character and willpower. There is also a large contingent of sex therapists who do not believe any sexual behavior can be addictive per se. Let's take a moment to review the definition of addiction in general terms, as it is used with regard to substances and behaviors, and see how it might apply to sex addiction or pornography use.

A Definition of Addiction

The American Society of Addiction Medicine (ASAM) provides a concise definition of addiction in two paragraphs. Let's begin with the first paragraph. "Addiction is a primary, chronic disease of brain reward, motivation, memory and related circuitry. Dysfunction in these circuits leads to characteristic biological, psychological, social and spiritual manifestations. This is reflected in an individual pathologically pursuing reward and/or relief by substance use and other behaviors."[4]

Here are the key terms. Addiction is a *primary* illness, that is, it is not caused by something else. It stands alone, and if other issues are also present, and these issues are treated, the addiction does not go away. Many people think just the opposite: "If we had only treated his depression, he wouldn't have gotten his third drunk-driving arrest." This common assumption is false.

Addictive disease is *chronic*, that is, persistent and recurrent. It can be put in remission with good treatment and ongoing support (such as twelve-step groups), but it does not go away. ASAM notes four areas in a person's life that are heavily impacted by addiction: the *biological, psychological, social,* and *spiritual* realms. In other words, addiction impacts just about every major part of our lives.

A person suffering from addiction pursues the substance or behavior *pathologically*. That is, they pursue it despite repeated negative consequences and often in opposition to their own beliefs and values. It is often called "a disease of the will," as it compromises our ability to follow our own best judgment—and our ability to eliminate the desire to stop the behavior entirely, as we read in the second paragraph of the ASAM definition:

> Addiction is characterized by inability to *consistently abstain*, impairment in behavioral control, craving, diminished recognition of significant problems with one's behaviors and interpersonal relationships, and a

dysfunctional emotional response. Like other chronic diseases, addiction often involves cycles of relapse and remission. Without treatment or engagement in recovery activities, addiction is progressive and can result in disability or premature death.[5]

Notice that the definition says *consistently abstain*. Many addicts can quit for periods of time, especially when they need to prove they are not addicts. They also suffer from *diminished recognition of significant problems,* which is commonly referred to as denial. It is important to note that denial is not stubbornness or irrationality. Denial is a symptom of the illness, rooted in the neurobiology of addiction, as opposed to a problem of honesty. The addict's brain is rationalizing and justifying in order to make sense of the behavior.

Most people would agree that Bill's experience with pornography matches up very closely with the medical definition of addiction. Deborah Schiller notes: "We know that porn is addictive. The level of neurochemicals that are released into the reward pathway indicates the person is addicted. Tolerance can be built up to pornography, just like any other kind of addiction. But the good news is, these patients can use the same tools that other addicts use to stay in remission one day at a time."[6]

Moral, Religious, and Spiritual Values

Moral, religious, and spiritual values do not figure into medical diagnoses. Such values may nevertheless cause significant psychological distress when an individual's behavior is opposed to their moral code. A person's sexual behavior may not rise to the level of compulsivity or addiction yet cause enough problems to require treatment. As with most problems, early intervention usually results in a shorter course of treatment and a more successful recovery.

"Jason" was the scion of a successful family in California and had every possible advantage while growing up. He attended Catholic school through twelfth grade and graduated with middling grades from a local university. During his college years he frequently went overboard with alcohol and other substances at his fraternity, but this was not his biggest problem. At the age of twenty-three, he admitted himself to inpatient treatment for pornography addiction.

Although he was nice-looking and had been lavishly supported by his parents with a new car and fashionable apartment, Jason had never had a girlfriend, either during college or afterwards. He socialized with women, but he was incapable of forming a meaningful relationship. He was not gay and was not troubled by gender-identity issues. No one knew the depth of his problem, as he carefully guarded his privacy. He simply seemed to be a polite young man who couldn't quite find his way. Counseling had been suggested to him, to work on general issues, and this gradually led to his willingness to address the big secret.

Jason's first exposure to pornography was at the age of eight. He had his own computer at home and had easily found his way to porn websites. There were no protections in place at the family home, so he had free access to anything and everything on the internet. He did not watch pornography frequently until he reached puberty, but he was mesmerized from the beginning.

By the time he was thirteen, Jason was watching pornographic videos daily in his room, both after school and at night. Other boys his age had discovered pornography, too, but they were not in his league. Jason watched for hours. When iPhones first came on the market, he was one of the first in his class to have one, and this put the world of pornography in his pocket. Early iPhones couldn't handle much in the way of internet content, but this soon changed, and Jason was drawn further and further into the dark world of online porn.

By the time he was in college, Jason was watching feeds from live webcams. Using his credit card, he paid for live-action pornography tailored to his fantasies. He watched porn videos throughout the day and treated himself to webcams at night. Jason did not know how to relate to young women his age. He could socialize on a surface level, but anything more was impossible for him. He did not know how to date or take the first steps toward intimacy, because his perceptions and understanding of sex were shaped entirely by pornography. On the few occasions when he did try to become intimate with a young woman, he was unable to perform. The shame and embarrassment of those encounters drove him even deeper into the world of pornography.

Before he entered inpatient treatment, Jason was unemployable, unable to form the most basic romantic relationship, and distant and secretive with male friends. He suffered from anxiety and depression, and only found relief online or using substances. He was a full-blown pornography addict, and he often used stimulants to stay up all night.

Inpatient treatment for Jason lasted ninety days. At first, abstaining from porn was tremendously difficult. He experienced a great deal of discomfort and sleeplessness, which only compounded his anxiety and depression. Gradually, however, the treatment process began to have a positive effect. He realized he wasn't alone, that others were going through the same misery of addiction that he was experiencing. He heard talks by people recovering from various forms of sex addiction, and this gave him hope.

Jason didn't want to live his life addicted to a screen and virtual partners. He remembered his early childhood when he was not enslaved by porn. He made a decision to follow all the treatment recommendations and make a better life for himself. Jason is in early recovery now and is committed to abstinence from pornography. He attends meetings of SAA (Sex Addicts Anonymous), and he hopes to explore a healthy adult romantic relationship once he has a full year of abstinence under his belt. He still has a long way to go.

Some people make light of sexual addiction, especially if they view it as a failure of willpower or morals. But we should not underestimate the suffering of the person who becomes truly addicted and has lost the power of choice. Schiller makes a pointed observation: "People who become addicted say they can't get aberrant sexual images out of their minds. Many wind up in psychiatric wards after serious suicide attempts, because it's such a terrible way to live."[7]

Effective Treatment Options

So what does good inpatient treatment for sexual addiction or pornography addiction entail? Not surprisingly, there are similarities with other forms of addiction treatment. I interviewed several specialists, including Greg Futral, the current director of the Gratitude sex addiction program at Pine Grove, to get the details.

The patient is assessed, and a treatment plan is developed focusing on three broad areas: biological, psychological, and social (abbreviated as the bio-psycho-social model). There is also an important spiritual component. The program in this sense is holistic, addressing the entire person. Here is an overview of the main areas.

Biological components of treatment: Sexual addiction is a compulsive activity, so it shares some of the brain pathologies of chemical addiction. Specifically, the prefrontal cortex, the supervisor of the brain and the seat of executive function, is effectively short-circuited and cedes control to the limbic system of the brain and the amygdala. This is what is meant by the phrase "the hijacked brain." Instead of our higher selves directing our actions, we are controlled by lower instincts and disordered desires. What is worse, we perceive these compulsions and desires not as wants, but as needs, like air and water. Our better judgment is curtailed, and we do things we know are wrong. This in no way absolves us of personal responsibility. We are not unconscious. However, this neurobiological perspective helps us make sense of our addictions and understand our unfathomable behavior. In this way, it helps point us toward a path to recovery.

Treatment includes education in the neurobiology of addiction and how to understand craving. Armed with this knowledge, patients are better able to understand how to maintain adequate support, so they do not return to self-destructive behaviors. Group therapy sessions help patients process the educational information and integrate it into their lives.

Psychological components of treatment: Both a psychiatrist and an addictionologist typically work with patients to address anxiety and depression—which are commonplace—and assess them for other co-occurring disorders. The treatment team must recognize contributing factors in the patient's life and address them in the treatment plan. These factors might include a history of family neglect or various life traumas. In many cases, a history of sexual or emotional abuse is present. Individual therapy will only begin to address these factors, and treatment for psychological issues will typically last longer than the inpatient treatment episode. Ongoing work with a specialist is often necessary.

Social components of treatment: People suffering from sexual addiction often have fractured social lives. They may have stressful, distant, or shallow personal relationships. If they are in a committed relationship, it may be on the brink of disintegration. They may find it hard to connect with others and to feel empathy. In most cases they will have difficulty on an intimate or sexual level, and may be virtually incapable of maintaining a meaningful personal relationship.

One of the goals of treatment, then, is to help restore or repair relationships. Patients are hurting in these areas, and group therapy sessions are helpful in establishing a connection to people who have the same problems. Being able to relate to other people, especially around a shameful issue like compulsive sexual behavior, is often easier than working on current family relationships. By talking through the challenges of their addiction and early recovery, patients begin bonding with their group members on a meaningful level, forming authentic relationships. These are the first steps toward healing and restoration.

Support groups are a critical component of treatment and recovery. These may include the various twelve-step fellowships like SAA, SMART Recovery, Celebrate Recovery, and more.

Professional services are important, but they are not sufficient. Mutual support groups are an invaluable part of the process.

The Healing Power of Our Spirituality

Our spirituality is a powerful force for healing. Tapping into a person's spirituality and helping them to develop a positive relationship with God (as they understand God) is often a challenge in treatment. Even people who have strong religious beliefs often feel deep conflicts in this area. They do not all fit the same pattern, but generally have one or more of the following features. As we shall see, these spiritual issues are common for most of us at one time or another in our lives. For patients struggling with addiction, however, they are crippling. Here are three examples.

A person may have been praying fervently for relief from their addiction but perceived that God did not help them. They were unable to regain control. Despite ongoing attempts to pray their way out of the problem, they have failed. The individual may then feel abandoned by God. Their prayers become hopeless, because their prayers are not coupled to constructive action.

A person with addiction may feel unworthy of God's help. They are so ashamed by their own behavior that they can barely pray at all. They are sure they are too sinful to be heard, so they feel forsaken by God. They may feel certain that they are too far beyond the pale to be forgiven or redeemed. They are in the wilderness and have nothing but their own broken willpower to fall back on. They fall into despair, and their feelings of unworthiness are redoubled.

The person with addiction may be angry at God. They may blame their abusive childhood, their fractured adolescence, or their hopeless adulthood on what God has or has not done for them. They may feel that God has subjected them to all manner of tribulations, which never seem to end. Pray for help? They see no point. They are in a blame game with God, and are quietly furious in their pain.

Again, any one of us may identify with these dilemmas at some time in our lives. When coupled with addiction and mental health problems, they can be multiplied exponentially. People in twelve-step programs often paraphrase St. James: "Faith without works is dead" (2:17). Overcoming an addiction requires both prayer and constructive action. A farmer may pray for rain, and rain is essential, but he must still plow the field.

Some of the greatest help for these spiritual maladies can be found in the various twelve-step fellowships. Here we will find people who have worked through these struggles and have been restored to sane and healthy lives. Twelve-step recovery is not a quick or easy process. But these groups are designed to help us clean up the wreckage of our past, deal with character defects, become honest with ourselves (and others), and become useful members of society once again. In short, these groups take people through a process that leads to a spiritual awakening.[8]

Programs like SAA call on a person to become more honest, open-minded, and willing. A person must be willing to go to any lengths to recover from their addiction. This includes attending group meetings, reading the literature of the program, working with a sponsor, working through the twelve steps, and ultimately, reaching out a helping hand to a newcomer.

Sexual Integrity: A Choice for Recovery

Coupling faith with a rigorous program of recovery can enable even those with serious addictions to overcome their problems and rediscover what it means to live with sexual integrity.

"Luis" is one case in point. Single and middle-aged, Luis watched pornography with some frequency. He did not go in for extreme videos or webcams, but he was still troubled by his own behavior. He stopped from time to time, but always went back to the easy release of porn and masturbation. He had no close relationship with women, and porn was an easy way to deal with his sexual urges.

Over time, porn became a daily part of his life. He did not like it; it went against his faith and his morals, and did not fit his picture of who he was. Luis had been in recovery from alcoholism for three years, and he was working a strong twelve-step program. He went to church every Sunday and found great meaning in the sacraments. Pornography was a spiritual embarrassment, but he was almost afraid to deal with it. What if he could not quit?

He finally decided to use the tools he had learned in Alcoholics Anonymous, combined with his strong faith, to confront his use of pornography. As Lent approached, he arranged a private Confession with his priest and admitted everything. He was going to make a clean break, and he asked for forgiveness and the grace to persevere. He had decided to give up pornography for Lent in a formal fashion, and he used his AA training to take it "one day at a time."

He later related that it was more like "five minutes at a time." The early days were difficult, but with effective prayer and help from his sponsor, he was able to string a few days together. He added some SAA meetings to his normal AA meeting routine. The battle became the focus of his prayer life, and as each day passed without a slip, he gained confidence.

It seemed almost impossible, but the days grew into weeks, and soon Easter was upon him. Luis had been abstinent for more than a month. He felt a new freedom and release from bondage. With greater faith, he committed himself to continued abstinence. He treated pornography with the same revulsion and wariness that he used toward alcohol and other drugs. The program worked. Whether he had been a true addict or not was of no consequence to him. He was free of the issue, and free to explore a more meaningful relationship.

Freedom Is Possible

Unlike drug addiction, with its external consequences, sex addiction is an invisible epidemic. It happens behind closed doors, though its effects are anything but secret. For young people growing up in an online world, porn is ubiquitous and all but impossible to avoid. Even church camps can be the site of first exposure, as kids are away from their parents but still connected to the internet.

The good news is that sex addiction, like all addictions, can be treated. Recovery is not only possible but probable, if only we have the willingness. Addiction is a chronic disease, but it can be put into remission. As with many chronic illnesses, keeping an addictive disorder in remission is a process that must ultimately be managed by the patient. Treatment and other people can help, but the sufferer must ultimately decide to follow an ongoing program of recovery. Jesus asked the crippled man by the pool at Bethesda: "Do you want to be well?" (Jn 5:6). The man did, and with the Lord's help, he was able to walk. Jesus asks the same question of each and every one of us today. Do you want to be well?

Questions for Reflection

1. In what ways has technology changed the ways we relate to one another? How can technology drive both connection and isolation? How does it exacerbate the dangers of pornography?

2. How does the neurobiology of addiction change the way you think about pornography, sex addiction, and your own issues with sex?

3. Addiction can cause a person to believe they've been abandoned by God. Have you ever had the same feeling? How did you overcome it and reconnect with God's love?

CHAPTER 4

THE JOYFUL DANCE OF
SEXUAL CONNECTION

TIMOTHY HOGAN AND KAREN HOGAN

Timothy and Karen Hogan have been on the spiritual adventure of marriage for thirty years. They have been blessed with three children. Tim's writing and work as a psychologist has centered on marital therapy for the past twenty-five years. Karen is currently completing her master's degree in spirituality and spiritual direction at Loyola University in Chicago.

Tim and Karen have worked together in therapy, training seminars, and on retreats to help people unlock the transformative power buried in the heart of marriage. In this chapter they offer couples practical pathways to grow and mature spiritually while also increasing the passion of their sexual connection. Their insights also provide a resource for those who work with couples, empowering them to explore the profound connection between spirituality and sexuality.

Thirty years of marriage have changed us in many ways, but none as strong as the way we relate to each other as sexual beings. From our initial struggles to integrate what we believed about God's plan for sex with our natural desire for intimacy, moving from a shame-based, biological understanding of our sexual desire into a grace-based, wholistic spirituality of sexuality, this journey of conversion has widened, deepened, and energized our understanding of the inextricable link between sexuality and spirituality.

Biological Drive vs. Sexual Purity

When we began our marriage journey, our spirituality of sexuality could best be described as an ongoing and often painful collision of our hot biological desire for sex with the cold waters of the Christian purity code. We both had spiritual conversions in college and, in retrospect, were a bit overzealous. Mutual friends introduced us to each other as "their two friends who were 'over the top' about God."

They rightly predicted we would have much in common. We went to Bible studies, prayed together before we held hands, and aspired to sexual purity. Early on we assumed that our sexual desires were fundamentally biological in nature and in need of both clear moral rules and strong self-control. We also both carried with us buried shame from our childhood and young adult life, and while these shame-based sexual attitudes effectively prevented premarital intercourse, they also prevented us from forging a deep and meaningful marital connection.

Fortunately for us, as newlyweds we knew where to turn for help. We were blessed with a rich Catholic foundation within which we could plant and grow our spirituality of sexuality. Both sets of parents were happily married and committed Catholics. We embraced the Catholic vision that marriage vows were powerful, sacred, and necessary before lovemaking made sense. And, while we failed to live up to every sexual ideal, we did wait for our wedding night to make love for the first time.

We also were blessed by a natural family planning (NFP) class early in our marriage. This deepened our understanding of Karen's fertility cycles and how they related to her mood and desire for lovemaking. In a world where so much of our lives was seemingly under our control, NFP reminded us that the sacred gift of life was not something to be controlled, but to be received as a gift from God.

Unfortunately, Karen's irregular cycles and markers caused us to struggle with the charting associated with NFP, and after discussing with a trusted priest friend how to balance the good of sexual union with the demands of responsible parenthood, we concluded that it would be irresponsible for us to rely solely on NFP during some seasons of our life. Yet NFP also awakened us to the profound health problems associated with oral contraceptives and the moral problems with abortifacient methods, and rescued us from the contraceptive mentality that was the norm in our community. In short, it gave us a strong foundation both to understand the miracle of fertility and to sort through ethical issues necessary to form our consciences.

We struggled in other areas, too. As Catholics, we had anticipated that marriage would be a journey filled with the joy of discovering each other's hidden beauty while simultaneously exposing each other's darker shadows and unhealed wounds. We expected this marriage journey to be a sacred calling, a "school of love" that would help us to transform and mature. In addition to our Catholic spiritual grounding, we also worked closely with Harville Hendrix,[1] with whom Tim did his doctoral dissertation. This experience intellectually prepared us to anticipate and embrace the joy of connection as well as the suffering that would likely come as we both faced our childhood wounds and sin patterns.

We believed in the purifying power of our sacramental marriage and that this suffering could be transformative, particularly to the extent that we could link it prayerfully to Jesus' suffering. We were right about the suffering part! Our early sexual relationship was a mild disaster. While we thrived serving side by side, climbing into bed with each other as newlyweds was often fraught with confusion, disconnection, and sadness. Karen frequently felt manipulated into lovemaking, while Tim would often feel intense irrational guilt, then withdraw and become distant after sexual enjoyment. In retrospect, we can see that our marriage was doing its job. As our desire to love each other awakened, along with it also stirred old wounds and feelings of self-contempt that needed healing. Put another way, sexual arousal often awakened shame that became a focus and catalyst for healing and growth.

Sexual Shame in Early Marriage

Tim's story. I had expected that once we were married, we would both feel free to enjoy a sexual relationship, unencumbered by guilt. In reality, we were both carrying burdens of resentment, shame, and guilt into marriage, robbing us of wedded bliss.

To start with, I had been sexually abused as a boy, at the hands of a beloved, trusted, and religious extended family member. Because of these experiences, I associated bodily arousal and the pleasure of being loved with a confusing fusion of powerful emotions. Whenever Karen and I aroused each other sexually, it triggered crippling waves of shame and the sense that what I was feeling was deeply wrong.

In addition, while I loved Karen very much, I had conflicted feelings about being married. For years well-meaning Catholic friends had noticed my love of prayer and spirituality and encouraged me to consider a vocation to the priesthood or religious life. Some even implied that the priesthood is superior to married life, pointing to select passages from the writings of St. John Paul II ("The Church, throughout her history, has always defended the *superiority of this charism* [celibacy] to that of marriage")[2] and St. Paul (that marriage is for those who would otherwise "be on fire"—see 1 Corinthians 7:9). This false notion that celibacy is intrinsically superior to marriage fueled my fear that sexual arousal, even within marriage, was somehow tainted.

Karen's story. My shame came largely from my dating experiences in high school and college. In my previous relationships with men, I had frequently felt pressured to go further sexually than I wanted. On several occasions I was nearly date-raped. And one day I overheard a close friend telling a mutual friend, "I only hang around her so I can get in her pants one day." This left me with a deep sense of betrayal and a fundamental distrust of the male sex drive.

My preoccupation with the danger of the sexual advances of the young men I dated caused me to distrust and to repress my own sexual desires. Talking with older, married Christian women who mentored me did little to help. Instead, I commonly heard these otherwise spiritually mature women insist that men simply have a stronger sex drive than women. It was not uncommon to hear these women (often after a glass or two of wine) say, "I don't care if I never have sex again!"

Once I became bogged down with the energy-stealing demands of raising children, I found myself avoiding sexual intimacy or submitting to my husband's sexual needs only grudgingly. Worries about pregnancy, sheer exhaustion, and my holdover inhibitions from past relationships all conspired to deplete my natural sexual drive. And yet, I also knew that my husband needed me—just as I needed him. And so we began a long, slow dance of intimacy, examining and releasing the burdens of the past in order to face the future God had planned for our lives together.

Holy Passion:
Reframing Past Assumptions and Beliefs

As we began working together through our sexual shame, we also began noticing how our Catholic world surrounded us with an elevation of celibacy and lack of role models for holy and passionate marital sexuality. The celibacy required of priests stood in stark contrast with the requirements of Protestant clergy, some of whom we counted as friends, who were married and thriving as professors and/or pastors.

One Sunday morning, as we sat in our traditional Catholic parish sanctuary, we noticed that we were surrounded by stained-glass images and statues of unmarried people. Sure, there were (and are) stories of people like St. Augustine who binged on "bad sex," then, after meeting Jesus, left their partners and children for a life of saintly celibacy. But where were the sainted married people with a holy and passionate life of spiritual and sexual intimacy? We were initially excited to hear that John Paul II decided to beatify a married couple until we learned that Luigi and Maria Beltrame Quattrocchi were, in fact, honored in part for their commitment to *celibacy* for most of their married life![3] Even more, none of their four children chose to marry.

In retrospect, we were looking in the Church for a truth more recently refreshingly articulated by Pope Francis in *Amoris Laetitia*: "God himself created sexuality, which is a marvelous gift to his creatures" (150). Unfortunately, we often struggled to find healthy role models and/or Christian dialogue about the beauty of erotic love.

Taking our previous sexual experiences together, we realized what we were up against: Our lives both inside and outside of church walls had left a clear message that sexual desire was an enemy from which we needed God to save us. Sexual desire was associated with shame and temptation, a drive that separated us from God. We were aware that we needed healing. And so, from the first year of our marriage, we explored our sexual history through spiritual direction, psychotherapy, intensive retreats, and plenty of small groups and Bible studies. What has emerged over the years is a thoroughly new and constantly growing spirituality of sexuality that is energizing our connection, exposing our need to grow up, and awakening a deeper spiritual discernment that makes our love more personal and transformative.

Four Paths of Conversion

Our sexual journey has moved us from experiencing our sexuality as a fundamentally biological desire to have sex that *separated* us from God, to a spiritual longing to love each other that *revealed*

God's presence within us. This desire to love each other includes, but is much larger than, our desire for sex. As we have reflected on this transformation, we have identified four interrelated paths of healing and conversion.

1. From Shame to Gratitude

While our journey of sexual growth and conversion has generally been slow and even cyclical (i.e., two steps forward, one step back), one evening in particular served as a sexual earthquake that permanently changed the grounding of our connection: We were moved from a place of shame and struggle to a place of grace and gratitude. Not surprisingly, it came in the midst of celebrating the Eucharist.

On a gloomy winter night in a rough Detroit neighborhood parish, we were meeting with a vibrant gathering of couples and their priest. We were there to teach at their annual marriage enrichment event. Prior to our workshop we celebrated the Eucharist together with all of the participating couples. When it was time to receive the Eucharist, couples were asked to stand side by side and receive as partners. The priest invited us to remember that our sacramental marriage, like the Eucharist, makes God's love visible to the world. We then went back to our seats, held hands, and silently prayed together. Something deep inside was beginning to shift.

The earthquake hit later in the evening. We were demonstrating an exercise we call "presencing," sitting face-to-face, eyes about eighteen inches apart. After praying for each other silently with our eyes closed, we then opened our eyes to simply be present to each other for several minutes. We were staying in each other's eyes, opening our awareness to the presence of God in the sacred mystery of one another.

On this occasion, as we looked into each other's eyes, tears began to flow for both of us. The incredibly deep and holy goodness of our sacred bond awakened, and the tears began washing away years of shame. We awakened to the way we had been embodying Christ for each other. The presence of God was palpable between us. The shame that had gripped our sexual desire was breaking. We began to see that our sexuality was bigger and deeper than a biological and lusty urge to copulate that required legalistic behavior management to make it morally permissible. Rather, our sexuality was a source of powerful desire to care for each other, to suffer for each other, to heal each other, to pleasure each other, and even to arouse each other. It was a desire to embody God's love with and for each other, to be a visible picture of God's love (i.e., a sacrament).

Then it hit us: God was not *against* our sexual desire. God was *in* our sexual desire. We were struck with deep gratitude. We could now see more clearly what it meant to call our partnership and our desire for each other a sacrament. Our love was, in fact, a visible sign of an invisible reality. In retrospect, we recalled our experience as newlyweds when we became houseparents for six developmentally disabled adults. Our love for each other expanded to build an authentic, joyful, laughter-filled, and restorative experience of family with these men and women.

Upon reflection, we saw this as a sacramental outpouring of God's love for this little community. Sure, either of us could have worked alone to supervise these clients and ensure a safe place to live. However, it was an outflowing of the joyful love of our sacramental union that created a restoring family experience for the residents. We now had eyes to see this powerful and godly love as an outflowing of our sacramental marriage.

Embedded in this seismic shift was a reorientation of what it meant to be sexually alive and to desire each other. We were inspired by Fr. Ronald Rolheiser's insight that the Latin root of the word "sexuality" is the verb *secare*, which means to be cut off with a longing to reconnect to the whole.[4] While this grace-filled reawakening of desire was noticeable with our lovemaking, most of the time our sexual desire was enlivening us to care for each other in practical ways that energized our love for our children and the people around us. In other words, our transforming love for each other was at work making us both better at loving the people around us.

During this early season of our marriage we developed a commitment to a life of prayer together that was grounded in gratitude. Following the Ignatian tradition of the Examen, we began a practice of praying at the end of the day, always starting with gratitude for where we saw God at work. This helped us to celebrate where God was working in us and guided us as we prayed for each other's challenges and adventures. We found this to be a particularly connecting practice when going on dates or romantic getaways. Soaking in gratitude for what God had been doing in and around us as we began these fun adventures helped us awaken to our deepest desire for each other.

We also found this practice essential in seasons of high stress and conflict, when the demands of family life and young children absorbed much of our attention and energy. We also became more intentional about making gratitude the center of our physical, embodied, and lovemaking connection. For example, inspired by the erotic poetry in the Song of Solomon, we began experimenting with naming the ways we desired each other. In addition to naming the ways we found each other sexy, we also learned to name the way our desire for each other connected to the rest of our lives.

For example, while massaging Karen's feet, Tim named his gratitude: "I love these feet. They have carried the weight of our children, they run the kids all over town, they bring the Kingdom everywhere they go. I'm so grateful that I get to be the one who massages them." This commitment to prayerful gratitude has been pivotal in our conversion from experiencing sexuality as a biological drive that would separate us from God into a spiritual desire that freed us to love each other with authentic and joyful passion.

2. From Self-Focused to Relationship-Focused

This seismic shift in our experience of desire exposed a need to face our self-centered patterns of relating with each other. Generally speaking, since Tim had spent most of his life as a young adult saying no to sex because he was waiting for marriage, he felt entitled to sex once we were legally married. This subtle and self-centered attitude of entitlement understandably triggered

Karen's fear that he was, in fact, just like so many of the men she had met in college who persistently tried to get her to bed. This pattern led Karen to either begrudgingly have sex or, more commonly, become emotionally and physically withdrawn. Even more, she feared that any physical affection (i.e., a longer kiss or hug or flirtatious comment) might lead to an expectation from Tim that lovemaking was now inevitable. So she was frequently cold toward Tim.

In addition to failing to love Tim, Karen also was failing to embrace the gift of her own sexual longings. Without owning and exploring the unique landscape of her undiscovered sexual desires, she had nothing authentic to offer our relationship. It was simply easier to avoid this whole area that caused so much pain, and instead she spent her efforts working to manage Tim's need for sex. As long as we saw our sexual desire as a disordered biological urge, and not a God-given gift, this conflict led to a downward spiral that was marked by mutual resentment and frustration.

As we awakened to the inherent goodness of our desire to love each other, we longed to break this stalemate. Our first step in conversion was to acknowledge our self-centered sin pattern and to seek each other's forgiveness. We then went about the task of breaking and transforming the lies about sexual desire that were seared into our minds as well as embedded in our bodies.

Thanks to the gifted ministry of our marriage therapist, we learned practical ways to create this loving, softhearted two-person system. For example, we created a discipline of giving each other full-body massages to teach each other the specific ways of touching that felt soothing and/or arousing. We then committed to not make love for at least a full hour afterwards. This discipline gave Karen permission and a safe space to awaken to her own sensuality, and gave Tim practice savoring sensual arousal for its own sake (rather than in a goal-focused way).

As our spirituality of sexuality continued to mature, this capacity to enjoy sensual arousal for its own sake was transformative and helped us to increasingly savor God's sacred presence within our family relationships. For example, not infrequently when our children were young, our romantic interludes were interrupted by sick or crying children. Rather than finding these interruptions only frustrating because they prevented consummation, we increasingly found it encouraging to playfully transform the joy we had stirred with each other to energize the love required as parents.

In a similar way, we began to more robustly integrate our life of prayer and life of love. For example, Tim found himself lamenting to his spiritual director that our infant son Brendan's nightly crying left him too tired to read the Bible and pray in the morning. Fr. Benno Kornely, his Jesuit spiritual director, suggested that Tim open himself to these nightly encounters and see in the eyes of Brendan our God who is weeping for the pain in the world. Tim came to see caring for Brendan not as something that kept him from his spiritual time with God, but as an invitation into a sacred space to connect with God and Brendan. Taken together, our transformation of sexuality, our longing to love, was expanding and energizing our awareness of God's presence in our love for our children, our community, and the world.

3. From Assuming to Embracing the Sacred Other

Over time we have discovered that to grow in our love for each other, we need to continually be learning about each other. This learning never stops. We have come to appreciate that authentic love is always specific and individual. This has meant letting go of the strong temptation to believe we know all there is to know about each other. Instead, we have learned to radically commit to the reality that we are both ultimately unknowable, a sacred other.

As newlyweds, we read secular and religious books that promised to reveal the secrets about how men and women were different and what it meant to be a good husband or wife. Often our well-intentioned, "theologically informed" attempts to show love to each other fell flat or, worse, backfired. For example, Tim had read that wives needed conversation. When he sensed that Karen had had a hard day, he would ask her to sit with him and talk about her day. It took us years to realize that this typically increased her agitation. Eventually Tim learned that, after a hard day, Karen feels loved when he suggests she take some time alone to journal or sit quietly beside him while reading or enjoying the night sky. Conversation is often not what she needs.

We have discovered that this willingness to embrace the sacred otherness of our spouse is the heart of our evolving spirituality of sexuality. We joke that we need to remember to study each other as a scientist studies an animal in the wild. Assumptions about what it means to love each other, however theologically informed or well-intentioned, often lead to increasing pain. Instead, we are committed to asking vulnerable questions and giving vulnerable answers. This allows us, over time, to become experts at each other, knowing better than any other person on the planet what our spouse needs to feel better when they are angry, sad, frustrated, or anxious.

We also get to be the ones who learn better than anyone else how they like to celebrate moments of joy and accomplishment. This is a practical way we have applied and seen the fruit of John Paul II's thematic emphasis on personalism.[5] We are most in sync with God's will when we learn to sacrificially see, explore, and love our spouse as a sacred being, made in God's image.

Tim: This commitment to learn to love each other as unique and sacred beings also required a transforming journey in our bedroom. The demands of raising three young children initially robbed us of our sexual connection, something we had only just begun to enjoy. And this change in our erotic connection was filled with riddles. For example, I could not figure out why Karen would rarely be interested in lovemaking even after a night out on the town with deep conversation and laughter. The reality? Physical exhaustion killed her sexual desire, regardless of her feelings for me.

Karen: I could not figure out why Tim was not more excited for lovemaking when I would surprise him after work with an empty house and an invitation to the bedroom. It turns out Tim likes and needs some time to look forward to connecting sexually. Deeply vulnerable and direct conversations allowed us to explore in more detail what we both found comforting and arousing, from how we enjoyed talking and touching, to fantasies that we had long kept hidden. This led to concrete changes. For example, when we planned special dates, I began scheduling a nap for myself so that I would not be exhausted at the end of the night. As the kids got older and stayed up later, we found it difficult to make love in a relaxed way for fear of the kids hearing. So Tim changed his work schedule so that he could be home one morning a week when the house was empty and both of us were rested. This became a coveted time for connection, and often, but not always, lovemaking.

4. From Legalism to Authentic Discernment

Our journey of living with increasing God-centered joy and passion has led to some dilemmas and tensions that have not been easy to resolve. Some of the questions that have arisen include, "What should we do with opposite-sex friends?" "What does it mean to be generously and responsibly open to new life?" and "What does it mean to mutually submit to each other?"

In each of these areas (and many others), we have found it transformational to actively apply the tradition of conscience formation. We began by studying what the scriptures said and why, then what the Church taught and why. Finally, we studied the relevant findings of experts. We brought this information into a process of prayerful discernment with spiritual mentors and with each other. Our goal was always to find the most honest, passionate, and sacred path of love. We believe that this commitment to conscience formation is not just an invitation, but a requirement. As the body of bishops agreed at Vatican II, our conscience is where we "discover the law inscribed by God to love, to do what is good and avoid what is evil . . . human dignity lies in observing this law . . . the person will be judged by it."[6]

One area in which conscience formation was particularly helpful for us involved friendships with those of the opposite sex. Many of our friends concluded that firm boundaries were needed to protect the marriage bond, and strictly observed the "Billy Graham rule," which says that a married person should never be alone with a person of the opposite sex. We didn't believe this to be the most realistic or prudent option.

For example, Tim spent a significant amount of time alone studying with Thea, a beautiful and godly female classmate who was a good friend to us both. On many occasions Tim and Thea would study for hours at our home alone, and many of our friends questioned us about why this was acceptable to us. The answer? Over the years we have developed a process of discernment regarding how to handle relationships with opposite-sex friends.

First, we talk openly about any friendships either of us have with someone of the opposite sex. There are no exceptions. In this case, we frequently discussed Thea's role in our lives and our role in hers. We spoke openly about her attractiveness and how that was affecting Tim. In the end we agreed that she was like a sister to Tim. Any artificially imposed restrictions would have simply poured cold water on a wonderfully warm and godly friendship.

Second, we long ago decided to give each other veto power over developing friendships with opposite-sex friends. For example, several years ago, Tim was working in a large group practice with "Terri," a young, talented, and attractive psychologist. He began discussing the possibility of leaving the large group and forming a new practice with her. As we prayed through our options, Karen had a strong sense that becoming business partners with Terri would be too risky; Tim's connection with Terri was robust and seemed to involve a personal connection beyond what would be needed to simply be good business partners. Because of Karen's discomfort, Tim agreed to stay in the group practice and let his friendship with Terri weaken. In this way we were honoring and protecting our sacramental partnership.

Third, we have agreed to avoid conversations with opposite-sex friends that would make each other uncomfortable if we were present. So, for example, if Tim is sharing coffee with a female colleague or friend and the conversation moves into a vulnerable area, such as our marriage or intimate feelings, Tim immediately asks himself, "Is there any part of this conversation that would be upsetting for Karen to hear?" If there is, he changes the subject and moves in a different direction. By intentionally and consistently applying these three principles, we live out the meaning of our sacramental marriage in a practical way, without resorting to rigid legalism.

Conclusion

We look back on our thirty-year journey with endless gratitude for the way our sexuality has transformed from an angsty and shame-ridden battle to control biological urges into a grace-filled, humbling encounter with God's invitation to keep learning how to love.

And our journey continues. Our marriage is still the epicenter of relational ruptures and repairs, and still requires a grounding in a life of prayer together. We also continue to need the delicious gift of "presencing": staying in each other's eyes for several minutes at a time, meditating on the sacred mystery of being in a sacramental partnership with someone who quite literally makes God's presence real.

As of this writing, we find ourselves on a new adventure together. Shortly after our last child left for college, Karen was diagnosed with cancer. For several months we have been spending much of our time together in waiting rooms, hospital rooms, or just sitting quietly in our family room while Karen recovers from treatments. And while lovemaking is temporarily less available for us, our sexual connection has never been stronger. The fruit of these years of spiritual and personal growth continues to multiply. There have been times when just the touch of each other's hand while waiting for treatment to start has moved us both to tears. Now more than ever we can taste what it means to live within the gift of a sacred vocation.

We continue to lean into these four paths of conversion.

1. *Cultivating a life of prayer together.* A shared prayer life, grounded in gratitude, continues to be our greatest source of

comfort, healing, and connection. While this might seem easy to sustain, it often isn't. We are surprised how often we need to relearn how to return to a rhythm of prayer together.

2. *Making our relationship a priority.* The effort we both put into making our relationship a priority constantly reminds us how thrilling, frustrating, and humbling it is to create a true two-person system. This process demands constant vulnerability and a willingness to continue learning about each other and asking for forgiveness when necessary.

3. *Embracing the challenge, the mystery, and the miracle of connecting with a sacred other.* This awareness, more than anything, stirs fresh waves of curiosity as we look to explore the undiscovered mysteries of each other more deeply.

4. *Meeting life's challenges with a commitment to conscience formation and discernment.* As Vatican II predicted, our world continues to grow in complexity. We are grateful to have a process that allows us to discern how to allow God's Spirit to guide us.

Questions for Reflection

Consider prayerfully and playfully conversing about these questions together. Remember that we deepen our sacred connection as we ask and answer with vulnerability.

1. What do we appreciate about each other? What qualities do we see that help us to notice God's presence in each other?

2. How did our sexual history help to prepare each of us for this journey? What blessings have been helpful? What wounds are still being healed?

3. How has our love for each other energized our love for the world? How do we make each other better? What small ways can we still make each other better?

4. What erotic memories of lovemaking still bring joy to our heart? In what ways have we experienced healing love through our erotic connection? In what small ways can we create more

space to explore the undiscovered landscape of our sexual desires?

5. What moral or ethical dilemmas are we wrestling with? What are some small steps we can take to learn, inform our consciences, and then prayerfully discern a better way to move forward?

CHAPTER 5

SEXUALITY, SPIRITUALITY, AND THE SINGLE LIFE

SUSAN MUTO

Susan Muto is cofounder (with Fr. Adrian van Kaam, C.S.Sp.) of the Epiphany Association and dean of the Epiphany Academy of Formative Spirituality in Pittsburgh, Pennsylvania. She has lectured all over the world and written more than forty books on the spiritual life, many of them coauthored with her friend and mentor, Fr. Adrian (1920–2007). Her latest work, A Feast for Hungry Souls, *is the culmination of a life-long love affair with the masters and mystics of the Christian tradition. In this chapter, she explores the calling God placed upon her life, as well as the blessings and challenges of her chosen path as a single woman in the Church.*

Growing up as a Roman Catholic woman in an Italian-American family in the 1950s, I was expected to follow one of two roads to fulfill my destiny: either to be married or to become a nun. These vocations defined what family members, friends, and my faith community saw as the best ways to show my love for God and others.

As far as I can remember in those pre–Vatican II days, priests and parishioners alike prayed for vocations to the priesthood, to the religious life, or to marriage. It never occurred to us to pray for God to call some to live the single life in the world. It was simply assumed that, outside of sacramental marriage or the vowed life in a community or clerical setting, a person would be hard-pressed to enjoy a healthy, wholesome balance of sexuality and spirituality.

There was also a vacuum of public support for singleness in the ethnic and secular world surrounding me as a young adult. Parents would never think of putting their daughter's picture in the local paper with the caption, "She is happily single." To qualify for this coveted publicity, a young woman had to be engaged. Stereotypes were difficult to shake. Not to have a Saturday night date led to the oft-repeated, oft-whispered question, "What's wrong with her?" This was often followed by the disbelieving query, "Does she want to be an old maid?"

The "unfortunate fate" of being single was seen as especially painful upon my college graduation. I was not one of the "lucky couples" who had found a mate for life. This lack on my part had nothing to do with my not liking men. To this day men are among my best friends. However, neither married nor religious life seemed to be the right fit for me. I was haunted by the desire to identify with Jesus of Nazareth, who remained a single person in the world.

And so I chose—despite persistent efforts at matchmaking—to pursue higher education. I had no time to shop around for "Mr. Right," to carouse in singles' bars, or to be lured into unloving, ultimately lonely relationships. I knew in my heart, to which the mystery was making its claim, that nothing would be more demeaning than forfeiting my vocation by succumbing to the dire prediction that I would never get over the misery of being unmarried and not having children of my own.

It took time to discover the meaning of this mysterious attraction to singleness, as an expression of loving fidelity to the Lord. Single by choice—not by circumstance and not in transition to marriage—was unusual but not impossible. After graduation from Duquesne University, I worked in the fields of journalism and public relations while going on to earn my master's and doctoral degrees in English literature at the University of Pittsburgh.

In the midst of these professional and academic pursuits, I experienced a seismic shift in the direction I assumed my life would take. In 1966 I met the colleague, mentor, and spiritual guide who most influenced my life and confirmed my calling, Fr. Adrian van Kaam, C.S.Sp. He invited me to join him in the establishment of a graduate-level institute of formative spirituality at Duquesne. In addition to administrative and editorial work, I discovered that my life's call would be to teach the ancient, medieval, and modern classics that comprised a two-thousand-year treasury of the literature of spirituality.

This work, begun in the university setting, came to fulfillment in 1979 when Fr. Adrian and I, along with many friends and supporters, cofounded the Epiphany Association. This nonprofit entity became the center of our full-time ministry and mission to the Church in the third millennium. From that point to the present, the Epiphany Academy of Formative Spirituality continues to serve the always-ongoing, in-depth formation needs of laity, clergy, and religious in a variety of faith groupings throughout the United States and around the world.

Called to Be Single?

Especially after I turned thirty, I continued to seek confirmation that the single vocation in the world was meant by God to be for me a permanent commitment. I still remember the day when one good soul told me in all sincerity to "bear the cross of my singleness for Jesus." When I reported this counsel to Fr. Adrian, he grinned from ear to ear and assured me that Christian singlehood is not a state to lament but a call to celebrate the gift of loving Christ in ways that transcend the exclusive obligations of married persons to care for their spouse and children.

"Love is the fundamental and innate vocation of every human being," wrote John Paul II in *Familiaris Consortio.*[1] My service of love as a single person might have been to those abandoned bodily, like the hungry and homeless, but I had a strong sense that God wanted me to tend to those abandoned in soul. If I had discovered the truth that no amount of worldly success could fill the inner emptiness I felt, might not others feel the same?

Fr. Adrian reminded me that the phenomenon of abandonment of soul affects everyone at some time in their life. My situation, as willed by God, was not single by circumstance, as in widowhood, or single in transition to marriage, but to be single by choice and to live this vocation in obedience to the teachings of the Church. I would feel abandoned by God if I did not abandon myself to God in my fully feminine sexuality and fully lived spirituality.

This leading of the Holy Spirit came to fruition when I wrote my book *Celebrating the Single Life: A Spirituality for Single Persons in Today's World* (1989). It covered such themes as experiencing limits and new horizons as single persons; being with and caring for others; and expressing singleness in word, action, and style of life. I shared my own experience as a single Christian woman committed to Gospel values in a world where careerism, consumerism, hedonism, and secular humanism tended to prevail. I refused from the beginning to the end of the book to define myself negatively—as *not* being married or as *not* being a woman religious.

Lacking the kind of formation offered in the clerical and vowed states of life, I realized how difficult it was to maintain sexual integrity as a single person in the world in a lifelong commitment congruent with the Church's moral tradition. Whatever our sexual orientation may be, we face the need for integration and integrity. As a celibate follower of Christ, mine must be a joyful spirituality that advances my own and others' faith in the goodness of God and that proclaims the graces that flow from loving chastely and generously.

Love and the Single Life

It is important for singles to show how and why sexual expression means much more than merely "having sex." It is to reveal in decisions and deeds how to be a masculine or feminine person radiant with self-respect and respect for others. It is to say no to irresponsible sexual encounters and yes to the art and discipline of loving others with the self-giving love with which God has loved us.

To separate sex from Christ-centered spirituality is to cast a shadow over the single celibate life as an expression of scriptural truth, doctrinal validity, and human integrity. We need to remember that we are born single and we die single. Before we choose any vocation—married or religious—we are one-of-a-kind human beings with unrepeatable fingerprints and unique genetic markers. Our essence in God, our being called by name before we come into existence, is the hallmark of who we most deeply are.

Is it any wonder that our human sexuality can never be reduced to mere physical genitality? We are more than our sexual drives for pleasure. Believers from time immemorial have channeled their sexual drives in order to attain a more transcendent understanding of the mystery of transforming love. Having Christ at the center of our love life entails refusing to treat anyone as an object of sexual gratification, opting instead to see sexuality and spirituality as integral components of our whole personhood.

We are not, nor can we ever be, a body without a soul or a soul without a body. We must reject this dualistic heresy and show respect for the sacred dimension of our sexual feelings and their expressions—for responsible, procreative love in marriage and responsible celibate love in the single life. Living in a relationship contrary to Church teaching holds no interest for single Christians, who choose to obey what the Lord asks of them: "I give you a new commandment: love one another. As I have loved you, so you also should love one another" (Jn 13:34).

There are pathways to celebrating the single life any sincere seeker can discover by embracing Christ, placing him at the center of all we are and do. As a Christian celibate man, Pope John Paul II exhibited a physical harmony, an emotional maturity, a superior intelligence, a compassionate understanding of young and old, and a strong personal commitment to Christ that inspired and renewed faith, hope, and love in everyone who met him. Years ago, when he visited the United States, he gave a homily on the Boston Common on October 1, 1979, with special implications for all those called to celibate love. He touched my heart when I heard him say:

> To each one of you I say therefore: heed the call of Christ when you hear him saying to you: "Follow me!" Walk in my path! Stand by my side! Remain in my love! There is a choice to be made: a choice for Christ and his way of life and his commandment of love. . . . Faced with problems and disappointments, many people will try to escape from their responsibility: escape in selfishness, escape in sexual pleasure, escape in drugs, escape in violence, escape in indifference and cynical attitudes. But today, I propose to you the option of love, which is the opposite of escape. If you really accept that love from Christ, it will lead you to God.[2]

Redeeming *Eros*

The forces fueling the sexual revolution and its effects on history and culture inundate social media to such a degree that single Christians have no choice but to be countercultural. Disciples of Christ, who are lovers of the Cross, cannot condone the pleasure principle, nor give priority to its egocentric demands. We must show deep compassion for anyone addicted to pornography, chronic masturbation, casual acts of immoral sex, and abhorrent treatments of the body God created. All such selfish gratifications lead to the dead end of sexual disintegrity, sadly accompanied at times by betrayed trust, culturally driven agendas, and defenses incapable of dialogue.

It is essential, then, that those striving to live this depth of spirituality in dialogue with our God-given sexuality embrace encouraging role models like St. John Paul II or wonderful single Christian women like Corrie and Betsie ten Boom, who countered the evil of Nazism in the West even as John Paul II, then–Karol Wojtyła, resisted communism in the East. I have had one such woman of grace in my own life, a vibrant single colleague, Marianne D., who fled Hungary after the revolution and spent her life counseling broken people, many of whom were addicted to drugs and alcohol and inclined to equate their worth with uncommitted one-night stands.

Dr. D. and I, inspired by the teachings of our mutual friend, Fr. Adrian van Kaam, often discussed the need to reform and transform the gift of *eros*, so deformed by sin and selfish sensuality. We also spoke as single women of the need to foster spiritual motherhood, understood as a mode of generativity beyond biological procreation that birthed new life in all those entrusted to our care as teachers and writers. It was Dr. D. who also insisted on our observing insofar as possible the "three 8s"—eight hours of sleep, eight hours of work, and eight hours of rest and restoration daily. Our conversations over the dinner table were an example of the recreation we needed to live a wise and balanced rhythm of spirituality and functionality.

Inspired by the spiritual mothers we loved, among them Teresa of Avila, Catherine of Siena, and Julian of Norwich, we agreed that celibacy was not a curtailment of our freedom but a catapult of sexual-spiritual energy that released us to live other-oriented lives sustained by prayer and presence to the Lord.

Our times together proved that one of the chief factors facilitating spiritual integrity for all followers of Christ is spiritual friendship. Soul mates, male or female, share the conviction that their best friend is Jesus of Nazareth, who lived the loving, self-giving celibate life they want to celebrate in one another's company. They thank God for the wonder of having found a person with whom they really feel understood.

The Gift of Spiritual Friendship

The classic Christian text on spiritual friendship was written by the Benedictine abbot Aelred of Rievaulx (1110–1167). I treasure this book not only because it details the incredible friendships Aelred enjoyed but also because it models the meaning of sexual integrity as a gift to the people of God. As Aelred proves from experience, such friendships begin in Christ, continue in Christ, and are perfected in Christ. The Lord stands between soul friends, so they never focus exclusively on one another.

By contrast, relationships that are carnal spring from mutual togetherness in behaviors lacking moral rectitude. Pseudo-friendships are often undertaken without deliberation, indulged in imprudently, are oblivious of how they affect others, and are governed more by passion than reason. Such contacts may be more worldly than wise, enkindled by hope of gain rather than by nonpossessive, inclusive love and other-centered service. Among spiritual friends, prudence directs, justice rules, fortitude guards, and temperance moderates.

Superficial relationships have the opposite effect. Idle chatter replaces honest conversation. The promises and commitments true friendships demand are quickly forgotten in more casual acquaintanceships. True friendship must be tested to be sure Christ is at the center, helping each person grow in mutual benevolence and charity. Such authentic friendships greatly aid us in overcoming self-centeredness, pride, and envy.

Aelred taught that in the presence of a true friend, we are able to unburden our minds; make sure that petty annoyances do not threaten our trust; and, best of all, converse about the illuminating inspirations we receive. He goes so far as to speak of friends exchanging a "spiritual kiss," not a meeting of lips but a mingling of spirits in an affection of the heart. Holding these friends together is the purity of their intention and their mutual practices of restraint and moderation. For Aelred, a friend is medicine for the ills of life and a sure foundation for growth in virtue.

To be rejected are puerile relationships embedded in fickle sentiment rather than in reason and faith. Encounters that despoil friendship tend to be reward oriented, overly loquacious, and all too often disloyal. To such types of friends we would hardly choose to entrust the secrets of our soul. From a true friend we receive loyal silence and forgiveness for our mistakes. There is no gossip between friends, only a renewed pledge to abide in Christ and to foster the intimacy that accompanies Gospel living.

Such love means being able to converse and jest together, to disagree with one another at one moment and learn something new the next. These exchanges and admonitions, honorable as they are, point to a higher standard of holiness: one that enables us to celebrate the blessings of our uniqueness within the common bond of our membership in the human family and in the body of Christ, his Church.

Moving Forward in Freedom

What are the obstacles to celebrating life as a single person in the world? Is it possible to be freed of the false guilt associated with the shadows of past indiscretions in order to fully pursue celibate intimacy with God and others?

For those who find that the pain of loneliness is unrelenting and does not evolve into the joy of solitude, the desire to find the companionship promised in marriage can be stronger than anticipated. It is tempting at these moments to rush into a decision we may live to regret. Rumbles of fear of the future without a spouse to care for us may grow louder. Silenced are the whispers of the Spirit, drawing us to the realistic awareness that our married friends and relatives may be going through similar turmoil— wondering if they ought to have remained single!

The reality is that both states of life share in the loving joy of the Resurrection as well as in the lonely sadness of Christ's passion and death. Christian singles can only be signs of redemptive love in this world if we have the courage to counter the stereotypes attached to this calling in order to find joy and purpose in our state of life. Think of the "plain Jane" who subsists on cans of

tuna and peanut-butter crackers, saying to herself, "What difference does it make when or what I eat? What's the use of treating
myself to a good meal in a fine restaurant where I'm sure everyone is staring at my table for one?" Or imagine the young man
who spends hours playing video games in his parents' basement,
unwilling to find his life's purpose for fear of failing or being
unable to fend for himself.

Habitual bad habits like these are the breeding grounds of
self-pity, anger, and depression, negative emotions that convey
the message that to be single is somehow bad. Such depreciative
attitudes obstruct the channeling of God's love to others. They
require an intentional course corrective if we are to be in the world
without being of the world. Only then can celibate Christians
remain open to the grace of the moment, willing to flow with the
gifts of God and the challenges they must meet to maintain sexual
integrity and spiritual inspiration. Viewing life through the lens
of celibate love as lived by the Lord enables single Catholics to
become the peaceful and peacemaking persons God calls them to
be in family life, Church, and society.

Healthy Habits of the Single Life

What are some of the other conditions that facilitate a sexually
and spiritually integrated life?

1. *Develop inner resources, especially a life of prayer.* These are
necessary to help us overcome all expressions of negativity.

2. *Reaffirm the worth and dignity of the single vocation* in public and in private. By their words and actions, single Christians
reverse the emphasis on rugged individualism and the "my way
or the highway" rhetoric of rampant narcissism.

3. *Maintain a posture of humble listening combined with a service
orientation.* Simple acts of self-giving prevent singles from succumbing to status and success as ends in themselves or falling
victim to self-centered preoccupations like sensual indulgence.

4. *Set aside time for explicit self-examination and a mindfulness
of all those in need of physical and spiritual care.* This wise blend of

contemplation and action offers us greater availability for ministry and gives heightened attention to the duty of the present moment—whether it means phoning a friend, visiting the sick, or helping others by the extra hours we spend counseling or teaching.

5. *Resist isolation and prejudice, and seek healthy forms of solidarity, support, and communion.* It is right and proper to resist instances of discrimination against single people in the workplace or at family gatherings, such as excluding or negatively labeling as "irresponsible" those who are unmarried. Similarly, single persons should assert themselves with those who assume them to be always available because they do not have a family, unreliable because they do not have to support a family, or potentially threatening to those who are married by virtue of their single status. One way to remedy the situation is to establish support groups to address issues of transitional, circumstantial, and permanent singleness.

6. *Seek time alone with Jesus.* At times single persons must go into the desert with Jesus, knowing that the test of their relationship with him is to endure dry periods in their prayer life. To persevere during these nights of pure faith requires emotional and spiritual maturity and a renewed commitment to live a Christocentric life with or without many consolations. Singles striving to imitate Christ are often surrounded with peers who choose to live together out of wedlock, who have left the Church, and who see no value in celibate love, sexual abstinence, or prolife Church teachings. Committed singles can effect necessary changes not by chastising others with a holier-than-thou attitude but by giving personal witness to the truth of God's unconditional love. By seeking reconciliation and renewal themselves, they encourage others to trust in the promise of new birth in and through the Spirit.

In an atmosphere where fragmentation, overwork, and burnout often prevail, single Christians can encourage others to take time to assess their calling. Rather than ask what the Church can do for them, it is best to ask what they can and must do for the

Church. The importance of gently yet firmly informing relatives, employers, and other Church members about the demands and delights of the single vocation in the world cannot be overstressed. It is also wise to convey the obligation to accept and respect the single person's need for privacy and solitude. Work and recreational choices, places of residence, and manner of living are decisions to be made with a respectful balance of distance and nearness.

We should avoid allowing others to direct us as to when we should work and rest, how to manage our time, and how to serve others in and around legitimate family obligations. A common concern arises when parents, perhaps with good intentions, begin to dominate the adult lives of their single children, notably when it comes to caregiving. Coercion is to be tempered. Freely offered choices are to be lauded. Many singles imprudently forfeit their right to arrange their own time because they cannot stand the guilt trips laid upon them by demanding parents or other authority figures.

We have to discern the fine line between those caring for us and those trying to control us. To touch without crushing or being crushed, to hold tight and know when it is time to let go, to receive the gifts of God and give them away—these are hallmarks of the single vocation. Contrast these values to the danger of becoming a single workaholic, who never says no for the sake of a greater yes. In a climate of functional accomplishment, where relaxation is associated with "weekend binges," it is impossible to be present to self, others, and God in an inspired, productive, yet peaceful way.

Singles have to learn by trial and error the discipline of exerting themselves, at times above and beyond the call of duty, while never neglecting the need to replenish their inner resources. It is not a luxury but a necessity to step away from the heated exertions of the moment in order to start again with renewed energy. Singles need an inner compass that directs them to cease doing something useful and to simply "Be still and know that I am God!" (Ps 46:11). Only when we distance ourselves from what we are doing and from the choices we are tempted to make, especially in the sexual realm, can we honor the need for creative, Christ-formed reflection and a serious assessment of our here-and-now situation. Once-tense thoughts may then coalesce into new constellations of meaning that lead to prudent conclusions protective of bodily, emotional, and spiritual integrity. Renewed, refreshed, and restored inwardly, we can give of ourselves outwardly to others in imitation of our Lord. Pledging to live our lives in service to Christ through the call to singleness does not mean we are obliged to develop an "Atlas complex," or succumb to the myth of omni-availability. We can only accomplish so much. Then we have to let go and leave the rest to God, offering a prayer such as this one:

> Lord, I sometimes feel like a wind-tossed reed. The world's a stormy place. I'm hurt by lack of understanding. I become harsh with others and then try to whip myself and them into a perfect mold, forgetting your graced mystery of formation. Then I think of you and your disciples that night on the lake. You calmed their fears as you calmed the waters and reprimanded them for their lack of faith. You showed them what faith really means by walking on the water.
>
> When I look at you, Lord, a certain peace comes over me. You have made me a unique person. My singleness is an unrepeatable offering of self through you to the world. In this moment of inwardness, I recognize anew the value of being who I am.
>
> Below the troubles of my mind and the emotional upsurges, I descend into the spiritual center of my soul. I allow myself to slip down, to let go, knowing that in this sacred core and center I am held, sustained, embraced by an Infinite Peace.
>
> Here, at the still point below all agitation, I am encompassed by you. In the peace of this moment, muscles relax; my mind is free of preoccupying thoughts; the whole of me is enveloped by your love. From this inner

peace there flows a willingness to reach out to others in service, friendship, and care. Nourished by your Word, held by your love, help me to become a message-bearer in the world, a humble servant of the mystery of divine formation.

Christian singles represent with their own unique style and intensity the purity of heart that enables us to taste and see the goodness of God. In a society that absolutizes power, pleasure, and possession, singles committed to Christ accept with joy their responsibility to foster the spiritual transformation of life and world. In so doing, they participate with single-hearted love in the redeeming plan of God for everyone who hears and heeds these prophetic words: "Do not fear, for I have redeemed you; I have called you by name: you are mine" (Is 43:1).

Questions for Reflection

1. Singles are challenged to see their state of life as a genuine vocation, as a specific human response to the perceived call and plan of God. How might your family and your parish recognize, affirm, and support people living this vocation by choice, by circumstance, or in transition?

2. Alongside marriage and family, and the vowed religious or clerical life, what complementary roles and gifts can single persons offer to family life, Church, and society?

3. Single persons bear witness to the inevitable incompleteness of life in this world. In light of this reminder of our finitude, have you ever pondered the truth that we are all born single and we all die single? Does this reality boost in some way your appreciation of singlehood?

4. Single people are ready, willing, and available for service as caregivers within reasonable bounds. How does the freedom feature of the single life, responsibly and chastely lived, contribute to the attainment of sexual and spiritual integrity?

CHAPTER 6

HIDDEN TREASURES
FOR GAY CATHOLICS

EVE TUSHNET

Candidly, and with a deliciously biting humor, Eve Tushnet shares her journey of self-discovery as a lesbian who eventually found a home in the Catholic Church in her book Gay and Catholic *(Ave Maria Press). She identifies the graces and challenges of that decision, the misperceptions many Catholics have toward members of the gay community, the temptations of self-hatred and despair that many men and women struggle with. She also identifies healthy models of same-sex relationships and the role of affection in sustaining life-giving friendships. She describes her quest for sexual integrity as a shift in focus from the avoidance of sexual sin to trust in God's unconditional love and membership in caring communities. Along the way she discovered that a life lived in harmony with the Church's teaching on sexuality can be joyful.*

Sometime toward the end of middle school, I was pawing through my sister's books in search of something to steal when I discovered a mystery I hadn't read before. I filched the book and settled down to read. The heroine was a lesbian—a term I knew from the progressive environment in which I was raised, but which I'd never considered applying to myself. I enjoyed her adventures and guessed wildly as to the identity of the killer. And then I stopped. The scene I was reading wasn't important to the mystery; it might not have been memorable to any other reader. But our heroine was having a beer with the woman she had a crush on. Through the narrator's eyes I watched this Texas blonde lift her long, long legs and put her boots on the table, tilt back the neck of her bottle, and swallow.

I recognized the narrator's attention. It held the same breath-caught, wordless intensity with which I regarded that one girl in my English class, the glamour queen of the eighth grade, with her olive skin and dark, tossing curls and her fledgling career as a catalog model. (I have simple, democratic tastes.) There was a feeling, like a key turning in a lock, and I recognized myself: *lesbian*.

This was not a traumatic realization. If anything, it came as a relief. My family had gay friends, and I was being raised more or less secular Jewish, without the terrors and judgments to which Christian gay children learn to subject themselves. (More on this later.) I came out to my best friend pretty quickly, and to my family shortly after. I spent high school as a queer activist, marching and postering and cofounding my school's gay-straight alliance.

My experiences in gay communities were just about completely positive. I'd grown up with great privilege; being part of a community that included people whose experiences had been much harder knocked a little bit of the arrogance off me. (Not enough, but some.) I learned that I didn't know everything. The very patient gay people around me taught me the tiny modicum of humility I would accept. I dated two girls; I'm grateful for their beauty and for their kindness to me, and sorry for the ways my self-righteousness damaged these relationships. In trying—however intermittently—to love and serve them, I became a somewhat better person.

In college I encountered, for the first time, Christians who showed me their faith in terms I could understand. I was shocked at how much the Catholics attracted me—the Catholics, but also and especially their Church, the doctrines of the Incarnation and the Crucifixion, the insistent physicality of the Eucharist, the sorrow and beauty to be found in even the most sentimentally furnished church. A friend once dubbed the place where we were baptized "the church where Snow White got married," but no plaster statue could hide the horror of the Cross or the ecstatic obedience of eucharistic adoration.

The Catholic Church's Sexual Ethic

I tried and failed to understand the Catholic Church's sexual ethic; I found myself willing to accept it anyway. It would be a stretch to claim that I understood what I was giving up. I was a college sophomore, a literal teenager, and additionally (and relevantly) an active alcoholic. I was an impulsive disaster with the self-awareness of a particularly foolish rock.

At that time I also had very little guidance. When I became Catholic, it wasn't just that I didn't know any other gay people who were willing to accept the Catholic sexual ethic. I didn't even know *of* any others. (I should have remembered that Oscar Wilde died in the embrace of Holy Mother Church, though I'm not sure his biography would have showered me with practical wisdom.) I accepted the advice I was receiving, which boiled down to

1. Learn a lot about theology to understand the reasons for the Church's teachings and

2. Don't date girls.

Those are fine things for a person to do, though it turns out that I wasn't good at doing either of them. I tried my hand at intellectual work, I did my time in the Theology of the Body mines; when it comes to chastity, I rely on confession more than self-discipline. (Chastity's hard when you live alone, man.) But this advice often made it *harder* for me to ask the right questions about my spiritual life. Slowly, and with many wrong turns that damaged my own life and others', I began to shift the way I understood my sexuality in light of my faith. I shifted from an individualistic focus on sexual sin to an approach grounded in trust in God and lived out in communities (Christian, gay, and Christian gay) that draw me into deeper intimacy with Christ and with other people. Over time I realized that sexual integrity cannot be lived in isolation; it relies on integrity in one's relationship with God, and it is strengthened by seeing others live with integrity within one's church.

The first thing I started to do right was to ask myself which aspects of my love of women could continue to shape my life as a Catholic. This isn't a question any of my mentors in the faith encouraged me to ask. They're great people who cared for me well, but they thought of my lesbianism as a sexual temptation that, like their own heterosexual temptations, needed to be resisted or even eradicated.

Many aspects of Catholic culture reinforce this narrow identification of "being gay" with sexual temptation. Progressive Catholics often assume that the only way to welcome gay people is to affirm gay marriage or to suppress all discussion of the Church's actual sexual ethic. Conservative Catholics often act as though simply being gay—or calling yourself gay, instead of saying you "struggle with same-sex attraction"—is a form of unchastity.

If you instead begin asking, *How can I express my love of the same sex in obedience to the teaching of the Church?*, you quickly find yourself out of step with the narrow orthodoxies of both progressives and conservatives. And yet this question opened my heart to forms of love and service I desperately needed. I realized that I longed to serve women, and after some investigation I began volunteering at a crisis pregnancy center, where I've served once a week for the past fifteen years. I longed for *intimacy, love,* and *care* in relationships with women, and I found that these words are not merely euphemisms for sex: they have their own beauty and reality.

A History of Christian Same-Sex Love

With aching slowness, I discovered the history of Christian same-sex love. This love forms part of the spine of scripture. It's the covenant made by David and Jonathan, and the promises of Ruth and Naomi. These loves have great spiritual meaning—Jonathan's willingness to give up his kingship for David, the sacrificial love for David through which he lives out his love of God, foreshadows Jesus' willingness to "tak[e] the form of a slave" (Phil 2:7). Ruth's love for her mother-in-law, Naomi, brings her into the Hebrew people in order to become part of the genealogy of all people's Savior, and foreshadows the spreading of the Gospel to the Gentiles.

This practical and spiritual love is echoed to a surprising degree in the vows of friendship made for centuries in the Christian West, in which two friends would pledge to share their household (*Wherever you go I will go, wherever you lodge I will lodge*), to care for one another's children and kin (*Your people shall be my people*), and to pray for the other friend's soul after death, sometimes sealing these vows by exchanging the kiss of peace on the church steps and receiving the Eucharist together (*and your God, my God*) (Ru 1:16).

These examples of sacrificial same-sex love reach their apex on the Cross, when Jesus gives his Mother into the care of John, "the beloved disciple." The intimate friendship between Jesus and John becomes a model for our own friendship with Christ. When Pope Francis instituted the feast of Mary, Mother of the Church, John 19:25–34 was chosen for the gospel reading, as if to show us that Mary is our mother *because* Jesus is our Friend. Scripture obviously uses marriage as an image of the love between God and human beings. But we've forgotten that scripture also uses same-sex love, adorned with promises and practical care, to teach us how God loves us and how we are to love him.

I first heard Ruth's promises to Naomi in a lesbian folk song. The singer's voice was low and tender as she sang, *Your people will be my people*, and then soared as she proclaimed, *Your God, my God*.

As I've come to know the beauty of same-sex love lived out in chastity, I've wanted to share this treasure with everyone, regardless of their sexual orientation. Gay people have remembered what most straight people seem to have forgotten: Same-sex love is beautiful. It's a necessary part of a flourishing community; it's part of a "parish ecology," in which many forms of love nourish and shelter one another.

As I've sought to deepen my own friendships, trying to model them more faithfully on Christ's friendship with us, I've begun to view my lesbianism not primarily as a source of temptation but as a source of guidance. Obviously everybody's sexuality is a source of temptation. (Even if you're good at chastity, that's a source of spiritual pride! So there.) The sexual element of my longing to love women is disordered, that is, it's a wrongly ordered expression or manifestation of a real and beautiful love. For many gay people, the best way to order our desires is to learn to express our love of the same sex well. To love women well means to love them chastely—but also, and more centrally, to love them devotedly, sacrificially, humbly, in obedience to Christ and modeled after his own example.

The Role of Affection in Same-Sex Attraction

God's love for us is not abstract. We were created with physical bodies for the same reason we were created with the capacity for thought and speech: to give and receive love. Culture and personality will color how much and in what way any individual person expresses and receives love through physical touch. I have friends who hug a lot, and friends who absolutely do not; I fall somewhere in the middle. For many of us these patterns are set in childhood. A friend who's very physically affectionate with his friends is just as cuddly with his sisters.

Because our contemporary culture tends to sexualize physical affection between adults, it can be especially hard for laypeople living celibately to receive the warmth and comfort they need. On the one hand, it is wise to avoid forms of touch that we have been taught to sexualize; on the other hand, viewing *everything* as incipiently sexual damages our relationships. If an American today saw the apostle John reclining on Jesus' breast, her first assumption might not be that she is seeing a teacher and his disciple.

And so learning to love others well in and with our bodies is complicated for everyone. It may be especially complicated for gay Christians, for we have so often been taught to fear our bodies and our desire for physical affection. It can be both frightening and humbling to ask for the touch we need. And yet it is so worthwhile because of the beauty and peace we experience when we find trustworthy friends who won't take advantage of us, with whom we can relax—as John lay trustingly against his Lord, our truest Friend.

Learning to give and receive chaste, tender physical affection often requires healing not only from lust but from fear, trauma, and lack of self-respect. The vast library of Christian advice to gay people on resisting lust, compared to the tiny amount of advice on unlearning self-hatred, suggests that most straight Christians radically underestimate how much trauma gay people in the pews may be carrying.

And so did I.

The Importance of Community

One of the most obvious ways in which gay communities have guided me in living my faith is by instilling in me a duty of love, though I have not always lived this duty as I should. Because my own upbringing was so gentle and I was so sheltered, I had no idea how much trauma many gay people have experienced at the hands of fellow Christians. As I've gotten to know more gay Christians, and reflected more on my own experiences in the Church, I've realized how devastating it can be to grow up never hearing about people like you from the pulpit *except* as threats to good Christians.

Gay Christians who want to follow Catholic teaching have no public role models—no Olympic athlete gives an interview talking about the support she received from her covenant friend, no movie explores our experiences without making sure we change our beliefs by the end credits, and even materials explicitly directed at gay Christians rarely consider our existence. In this silence, our friends and mentors can't learn how to love and shepherd us; and how can we learn, in total isolation, how to love God?

Most of the gay people I've spoken with who are seeking (or sought in the past) to live in harmony with the Church have been encouraged to try to become straight. They've often been told that this is the only right path for them. And this has seemed plausible, since they see no future for a gay person in the Church. It's hard to imagine yourself doing something when you don't know anybody else who ever has.

Many of the gay Christians I know have lost jobs or ministry positions because they were honest about being gay. (This includes many, many people who were clear that they accepted their church's sexual ethic.) Most of the gay Christians I know have been taught to fear any same-sex friendship that became "too" intimate, too close—too loving. Shockingly, teaching people to cauterize their hearts doesn't make love of God easier. But it took me a long time to realize how badly isolation, suspicion, and silence had damaged gay people's relationships with God.

Out of my naivete I made a lot of bad decisions, especially in my priorities—which actions and arguments I considered most important. I focused on telling other gay people what we shouldn't do, not on listening and understanding all the barriers Christians had placed between gay people and the Gospel. I'm sorry for that, and my own experience has convinced me that most Christian witness to gay people must include apology and humility.

Conservative Christians often treat gay communities as a threat. Gay people in the churches are encouraged to separate themselves from gay communities, including those communities that helped and sheltered them in the past. The language of "struggling with same-sex attraction," while it describes some people's experiences very well and is helpful to them, should not be imposed or demanded by straight people. It focuses on sexual temptation in a way that easily obscures the possibility of same-sex love; and it is often used to separate people from gay communities in which they might find support and understanding.

I've been so grateful for the gay communities (many of which are also Christian communities) in which I've participated. These communities often preserve a robust understanding of "chosen family," or friends as kin. "Chosen families" are a form of mutual sacrifice often undertaken out of necessity, by people who have been rejected by their families of origin. Some gay communities can be havens for the rejected—something our churches should be. Unfortunately, much of this rejection is inflicted by Christians, the very people who should be the safe harbors.

For a long time I would say, casually, that I wasn't raised Catholic so I don't have "a lot of that baggage." And one day I noticed what I was really saying: I wasn't raised Catholic, so it was *easier* for me to trust God's love than it is for most gay people raised in the Church. What an indictment.

At the heart of sexual integrity is precisely this trust in God. When I became Catholic, I was told to be chaste; because I was gay, people told me *a lot* about chastity. Nobody (myself included) wondered whether, as a lesbian, I might need extra instruction in trusting God's unconditional love. And yet as I get to know more gay Christians, I've found that the single greatest and most widely shared temptation we face is not lust. It's despair.

The Temptation of Despair

Despair can manifest as a feeling of emptiness, aloneness, a feeling that we are uniquely cut off from God despite every effort to get back to him. It's a feeling of eternal and existential singleness: unyoked, unloved. Where obedience is attempted, it's attempted without any trust in the covenant between God and the soul, and so obedience becomes a form of self-harm. Obedience and disobedience feel equally like failure. You come to see God as a probation officer always looking for reasons to condemn you, or as a disappointed parent whom you feel you are letting down simply by being honest about what you are experiencing.

Despair feeds lust—after all, if you hate yourself and can't bear to contemplate your life, your efforts at self-medication may turn your phone into a tiny porn dispenser! Sadly, the remedies gay Christians are given for lust only feed the despair. We're told to flee deep friendships because they might be near occasions of sin; we're encouraged to isolate ourselves and to speak in harshly negative terms about our longings for love and intimacy. Our sexual sin is often driven by trauma, shame, or fear, and yet these terms are rarely used to name the root causes of our unchastity—instead we're treated as if our homosexuality is the root cause.

Even in the confessional, desperately in need of the truth that we are loved, the priest corrects us when we call ourselves "gay." He says, "No, you are a beloved daughter of God"—and the lesson here is that those are opposite things. So even this reminder that our soul is still wedded to Christ and he is faithful, is twisted into the lie that we are loved *because we're not really gay.*

Despair is spiritual slavery. And by far the most common way for gay Christians to liberate themselves from this slavery is to reject the Catholic sexual ethic. Every gay Christian I know can cite examples of people who were in despair until they rejected Christian sexual discipline, and now they are self-accepting, joyful, freed. I have learned, however, that a life lived in harmony with Catholic doctrine can also be joyful.

I have learned that celibacy can be a haven for love: love of other people and love of God, who comes bringing light into the hushed and darkened bridal chamber of the heart. I have learned that honesty about my desires and my community strengthens my faith, rather than threatening it. I have learned that God's love doesn't wax and wane with my own virtue—that he is strong where I am weak, that he is faithful and good even when I'm a reprobate out of an old-school jukebox country song. I have learned that God loves gay people so much that he has let our communities cherish certain truths that mainstream Christians have lost, so that we can return to the churches with our hands full of gifts.

I have also learned that this perspective is rare.

I have learned that many gay people were taught very different, much harder lessons in their churches: a backward catechism, where *Why did God make you? God made me to know him, to love him, and to serve him in this world, and to be happy with him forever in the next* has been replaced with, *Why did God make you like that? God made me like this because I do not know him, because I cannot love him, because there is no way for me to serve him in this world (whether in marriage or in religious vows), and because he will be unhappy with me forever unless I'm fixed.*

Christian Sexual Integrity

Sexual integrity, under these conditions, cannot be defined simply as the absence of obvious sexual sin. What looks like chastity from the outside may be a brittle, traumatized despair, or an attempt to earn God's love. (And unchastity may be part of a long journey of unlearning the backward catechism. Where that journey leads may depend, in part, on how confessors, parents, and other Christians treat the sojourner.)

Christian sexual integrity is a form of union, beginning with the individual soul's communion with her Lord. Communities that practice welcome and mutual sacrifice can help to build the walls that shelter this encounter with Christ. A community that is living sexual integrity is a community in which straight and gay people sacrifice for one another. It's a community in which the many forms of Christian love reinforce one another: where monks pray for families, where single moms live in community with celibate laypeople, where friends are kin. It's a community in which Christians stand with gay people when we're targeted for abuse, whether that's physical violence, workplace discrimination, or familial rejection. Christian sexual integrity looks like Gabriel Salguero, an Assemblies of God pastor who opened his church to give blood, host funerals, offer grief counseling, and rally in prayer after the 2016 mass shooting at the Pulse nightclub in Orlando.

Christian sexual integrity does *not* look like, and in fact is betrayed by, the many pastors and Christian employers who have fired (orthodox, obedient) gay workers simply for coming out or being outed. The volunteers at St. Louis Pride who stand along the parade route in the sweltering sun handing out water bottles with the message, "*You matter*—Jesus" are living sexual integrity, not solely because many of them are chaste LGBTQ+ Christians but because they are Christians who treat *all* LGBTQ+ people as beloved by God. Sexual integrity requires solidarity—not erasing our differences, but serving and sacrificing for one another.

Individual sexual integrity rests on the assurance that no one is single—all of us have a Lover who is more faithful than we could ever hope. Communal sexual integrity rests on practices that help ensure that no one *feels* single—that the love of Christ is experienced on a daily basis at home, at work, and in the street. No one lives individual sexual integrity perfectly. Our communal sexual integrity is even rarer, requiring an even deeper surrender to God. It is also, for this reason, more precious.

Questions for Reflection

1. When have you found yourself giving and receiving love in unexpected ways? What are the most intense nonsexual relationships in your life, and how do you express and receive love within these relationships?

2. What messages about gay people did you receive from your family, from priests, and from other teachers within the Catholic Church? What did this early formation in the faith teach you about gay people's relationship with God?

3. Where have you seen devoted same-sex love in your own life or in your church? Is this something you long for? Who are your models for self-giving, same-sex love (whether people you know personally, saints, or fictional characters)? What do these relationships teach you about God's love?

4. If you decided to serve gay communities in your area by performing the corporal works of mercy, where might you start? Who would you talk to, in order to find out what is needed?

CHAPTER 7

GROWING IN SEXUAL INTEGRITY
AS A CONSECRATED MAN

DANIEL KEATING

Daniel Keating is a professor of theology at Sacred Heart Major Seminary and a member of the Servants of the Word, an ecumenical, charismatic, missionary community located in Ann Arbor, Michigan. He writes with deep insight, realism, and conviction as he describes the relationships, virtues, and practices that mark the path to sexual integrity in the life of men who, in responding to the call and grace of God, choose to live a consecrated life in community.

M y community of brothers, the Servants of the Word, is one of many new forms of consecrated life that the Spirit seems to have called into existence today.[1] A lifelong Catholic and a product of Catholic schools, I experienced an awakening of my faith in college along with a clear sense of being known and called by God. As I considered the question of vocation over several years, I began to pursue participation with—and eventually found a home among—the brotherhood of men with whom I have lived these past forty years.

Following my own period of formation and discernment, I served for fourteen years as our director of formation (the novice master), working closely with many young men as they sought to discern God's call upon their lives. It is from my own experience of walking this path to sexual integrity—and of accompanying many others on the same path—that I offer whatever wisdom I may have.

The topic I was asked to address, sexual integrity for a consecrated man, immediately raised two questions in my mind. The first is, "How is sexual integrity distinctive for a consecrated man, in contrast to what it means for men and women in any state of life?" The second is, "How does a consecrated man's sexual integrity influence the way he lives his entire life—a life that has many essential elements woven together into one whole?"

My conviction regarding the first question is that the path to mature sexual integrity is largely *common* to all men and women, in both the married and celibate states. While distinctive vocations have particular needs and strategies, each with special obstacles to overcome, we are all called to deep conversion (which serves as the foundation), to chastity in mind and body. In short, each of us is called to be transformed in Christ—and this transformation process produces in us a mature, integrated sexuality.

My aim here is to speak to the distinctive ingredients that mark the path toward mature sexual integrity for a consecrated man. Sexuality cannot live and thrive on its own. It must be embedded in a wider way of life and a network of relationships. And so I hope to illuminate that wider context within which a healthy celibate life can flourish before offering a more thematic description of what I believe to be core elements that make up a life of sexual integrity for a consecrated man.

The Call to Conversion and Discipleship

I would not know how to begin addressing the topic of sexual integrity, or know how to counsel someone in it, without a solid foundation in place. As the parable about the man seeking to build a house shows us, we need to build this house upon a foundation of rock, not of sand (see Luke 6:48).

The foundation I am referring to is *the call of Christ* and *the response of full conversion of heart and mind*. Included in this is the determination to set out on the road of committed discipleship. This may seem to be asking a lot right at the start, but this is what the gospels describe as the path of discipleship, and in my experience this conversion of life and full submission of mind and heart as a disciple are essential for the growth of sexual health and integrity.

There are no doubt many causes for the present sexual abuse crisis, but one main reason for this enormous deficit in upright and holy conduct is a lack of full conversion and commitment to discipleship right from the beginning. If the foundation is not well laid—if the heart and mind aren't fully submitted to God's Word and docile to the work of the Spirit—then we will not see the fruits of mature sexual behavior in the lives of the faithful.

Paul couldn't be clearer about the need for building this living foundation in the lives of believers and in the Church as a whole: "According to the grace of God given to me, like a wise master builder I laid a foundation. . . . For no one can lay a foundation other than the one that is there, namely Jesus Christ" (1 Cor 3:10–11).

Once this foundation is laid, Paul instructs in his letter to the Ephesians, we must continue to build by operating in the gifts of the Spirit "to equip the holy ones for the work of ministry, for building up the body of Christ, until we all attain to the unity of faith and knowledge of the Son of God, to mature manhood, to the extent of the full stature of Christ, so that we may no longer be infants, tossed by waves and swept along by every wind of teaching" (Eph 4:12–14). In order to live the truth in love, especially with regard to sexuality, Paul encourages the faithful to "put away the old self of your former way of life, corrupted through deceitful desires, and be renewed in the spirit of your minds, and put on the new self, created in God's way in righteousness and holiness of truth" (Eph 4:22–24).

This is not just high-sounding religious jargon or old-fashioned piety; it is a statement of deep conversion of mind and heart, true submission to Christ, and commitment to remain on the way to full, mature discipleship, what Paul calls "the measure of the full stature of Christ" (Eph 4:13).

To say this differently, sexual wholeness, peace, and righteousness is not a single blossom in someone's life that can appear all by itself. It is the product of a *whole* life submitted to God, energized by the Spirit, that eagerly seeks to follow the wisdom of God in all aspects of life. For many young Christian men and women, the path to sexual integrity and uprightness is a long and difficult one, even for those who have laid a solid foundation. But without this foundation, chances of arriving at sexual integrity according to the Gospel are slim. With this foundation in place, the ingredients are there for someone to make consistent progress—with the help of friends and counselors—on the road to sexual integrity.

For the Christian, sexual integrity derives its meaning not from any cultural construct, not from individual notions or preferences or impulses, but from *God's* design. "The successful integration of sexuality within the person" (*CCC* 2337), body and spirit, thrives when it follows the wisdom of God as given in the narrative stories of the Bible, in the commandments, in the explicit teaching of Jesus, and through the wisdom of the Church. When we live out our sexuality according to God's created purposes, as described and governed by the revelation of scripture and by the Church's perennial and present teaching, we find true freedom and peace.

The Healing Work of the Spirit

Anyone who has earnestly sought to live the Church's teaching about sexuality experiences real and ongoing challenges. It is one thing to know how we are to live, but another to actually live it successfully and peacefully. The major challenge that most men face stems from the ingrained habits of sexual misbehavior that they develop in adolescence and early adulthood. But underlying these habits is a nature wounded by sin, such that we experience desire for sexual fulfillment in ways that deviate from the plan and purpose of God.

The enormous accessibility of online pornography today reveals both our misplaced desires and our ingrained habits of sin. Certainly a change of mind—a conversion of the intellect—is a crucial and necessary step in advancing toward sexual peace and integrity. But even when we have gained ground through the application of our will and the wisdom of good practices, we need a source of power and transformation beyond the exercise of our intellect and will. In short, we need to learn to walk in the power and freedom that the Spirit brings.

For those confused about how to walk the way of sexual integrity, the Spirit speaks to our hearts and reminds us of the truth: "The Advocate, the holy Spirit that the Father will send in my name—he will teach you everything and remind you of all that I told you" (Jn 14:26). Our inner counselor prompts us to pursue the path of purity—though of course we must choose to walk in that path.

When strong, wayward sexual impulses are, humanly speaking, too difficult to resist, we must call upon the Spirit, who genuinely purifies our hearts and minds and desires. This isn't just internal strength to resist sexual impulses. The Spirit enables us to see ourselves and each other from God's perspective, allowing a true healing of our sexuality. The Spirit has the power to heal, through prayer and deliverance, those of us who have been deeply wounded in our sexuality—wounds we may bear either through things we have done or (very often) through things done against us.

Living with sexual integrity includes keeping God's commandments, but it is much more than this. For a consecrated man it means progressing to an experience of life where we are at peace with our own sexuality and where we see the beauty of God in the sexuality of others—and we are free to relate to others with appropriate affection and friendship. This experience of sexual peace and wholeness will never be perfect in this life—struggles and imperfections will always remain to a degree—but through our cooperation with the varied work of the Spirit, over time we can experience substantial freedom and peace in our sexuality and in the wide variety of relationships that we as consecrated men are called to embrace.

Testing a Vocation: Gaining Confidence and Strength

As mentioned previously, many of these principles of sexual integrity apply to everyone, men and women alike: a deep conversion of mind and heart, a commitment to set out on the path of discipleship, and the progressive healing of our sexuality through the work of the Spirit as we live out our lives in friendship with others.

For those considering a vocation in the consecrated or religious life, these principles are also prerequisites to testing the calling to consecrated celibacy, setting aside their life for God alone. This testing is a crucial part of the direct engagement with God himself, akin to a time of courtship between a man and a woman. Many of us, as we face this time of discernment, would prefer a voice from heaven telling us what to do. In short, we would like someone else—namely, God—to make the decision for us by fiat, thus relieving us of the hard task of sorting through many things and wondering whether we are on the right track.

But to wish for this is to miss the very great privilege and dignity that the Lord God gives to each of us, when we actively cooperate in the selection of our vocation and meet God's grace with our own responsive yes. To receive a voice from heaven telling us what to do is in fact a weak and fragile form of discernment. It relies on one intervention and does not involve our own engagement in the choice or the progressive transformation that occurs in us as we consider a consecrated vocation. It is by going through a lengthy, disciplined process of discernment that we receive the full fruits of what God has for us. The process is part of what prepares us for this vocation, and our active cooperation with grace teaches us how to live that life going forward.

Furthermore, there is a great dignity in finally *choosing* to live for God in this way. The decision to follow a consecrated vocation is not just a deduction from data, but a fully orbed *choice* that says, "I choose to set aside my life for the Lord, and I expect to receive his help and his grace, and I do this freely and with my full heart because of the conviction that God has called me to this life and shown me that I have the help and grace available to enable me to live this life peacefully and well."

This period of discernment is critical for moving toward sexual peace and integrity for two reasons. First, it is only by testing our ability to live fruitfully apart from marriage and family that we come to know that we are in fact well equipped for this. The time of discernment provides the testing ground for whether we will flourish in the soil of consecrated celibacy. Second, it is crucial that our decision to live a consecrated life engages our whole heart, mind, and will. Troubles will come; temptations may knock at the door; new issues might arise and shake our confidence. If we are going to weather these storms, it is critical for us to know that we have given ourselves fully to the Lord, with the free assent of our heart and will.

If the discernment process is not properly carried out, or if the decision for consecrated life is made half-heartedly, then the potential for the future undermining of confidence in the vocation grows considerably. But when we walk the path of discernment with focus and faith, honestly facing up to the weaknesses and shortcomings that necessarily are revealed in the process, then our clear and free decision to set apart our lives for Christ is grounded securely. The issues we have faced and overcome will give us confidence to face whatever future challenges might arise. We know, with eyes wide open, that we have handed over our lives to God, and can confidently trust in his grace to help us walk in this path faithfully for the rest of our lives.

Elements of a Fruitful Consecrated Life

What are the basic components that must work together for a consecrated person to grow toward—and achieve—sexual integrity? Of course, there are a variety of forms of consecrated life, both ancient and new, in the Church today. Each form has its own pattern for daily living and its own gathered wisdom for how to live faithfully for Christ in the midst of the many challenges presented by contemporary society. Nevertheless, there are common elements that apply to nearly all those seeking to live a consecrated life, even if each particular expression of consecrated life contains its unique synthesis of these elements.

1. Prayer and Friendship with God

A consecrated vocation makes no sense if prayer and friendship with God are not at the center of things. I phrase this element as "prayer and friendship with God" in order to include both the patterns of formal and informal prayer *and* the genuine underlying friendship-relationship that is the wellspring and product of a consecrated life activated through regular prayer. Both the pattern of prayer and the genuine relationship with God are essential. Without patterns of prayer, relationship with God loses its solidity and withers; without a genuine friendship, prayer becomes an external and brittle shell practiced for its own sake. It becomes a branch detached from the vine.

Do prayer and friendship with God bear directly on growth in sexual integrity for a consecrated man? Most certainly. Prayer is the fount of life for every Christian, whether married or single. But for a man (or woman) who has set aside the great good of marriage, prayer becomes even more central. When a man chooses to refrain from a sexual relationship and from all the other relational riches that are included within the covenant bond in marriage, his relationship with God takes on a greater and more significant role.

As we know, the marriage relationship, including the aspect of sexual union, is a central biblical image pointing to the even greater nuptial relationship between Christ and the Church, and Christ and the individual person. When we choose to refrain entirely and for the whole of life from a sexual relationship, this puts the spotlight on our relationship with God. It's not that the one is a simple substitute for the other: one's relationship with God provides both more and different fruits than a sexual relationship.

Our intimacy with God, and the profound inner changes that this can bring about, exceed what any human relationship can provide. At the same time, a relationship with God does not provide everything that a human sexual relationship supplies. For a consecrated man or woman, then, there are great gains but real and genuine renunciations—and these are clearly felt, at some times more intensely than others. In fact, it is this experience of a "lack" or "absence" that can be a powerful impetus toward prayer and deeper friendship with God. Yves Raguin captures the positive role for solitude well:

> Those who have renounced marriage experience very keenly the pain of solitude, not only physical solitude, but, more still, solitude of heart. This feeling can be joined to a deep union with God. In fact, solitude is necessary for the growth of celibacy that is the love of Christ and of men. . . . One must learn to live with, indeed desire this solitude, because it is essential to the growth of love consecrated to God.[2]

Several of my own deepest times of unscheduled prayer occurred when I was experiencing the cost of my vocation on the human level. This pushed me to seek the presence of the Lord and draw from him both strength and solace. As human beings made in the image and likeness of God, we were made for communion with God and others, including the profound bond of union in marriage. When we choose to set aside this experience of deep union of body and soul, there is a real lack that we are bound to seek a remedy for in one way or another.

If I have renounced a sexual relationship *and* my prayer life is either shallow or merely formal, I will almost certainly look elsewhere to fill this lack in my life—and these substitutes will not yield a life of healthy, integrated sexuality. But if I am seeking God, if I am making my way into his presence, then God will be for me what I both need and desire. Here the psalms of longing and yearning for God play an important role for a consecrated man. They provide a "dwelling place," a means of expressing what the Lord God is meant to be for him in a life of consecrated celibacy, as the following examples display:

> O God, you are my God—
>   it is you I seek!
> For you my body yearns;
>   for you my soul thirsts,
> In a land parched, lifeless,
>   and without water. (Ps 63:2)

> As the deer longs for streams of water,
>   so my soul longs for you, O God.
> My soul thirsts for God, the living God.
>   When can I enter and see the face of God? (Ps 42:2–3)

And while there is an element of yearning for God from the experience of what a consecrated man lacks, there is at the same time a *delight* in God that yields a life of joy and fulfillment, as expressed in these verses from Psalm 73:

> Whom else have I in the heavens?
>   None beside you delights me on earth.
> Though my flesh and my heart fail,
>   God is the rock of my heart, my portion forever. (Ps
>   73:25–26)

In short, prayer and friendship with God are at the heart of consecrated life. Growing in prayer and divine friendship is essential for sound, healthy, integrated sexuality.

2. Friendship within Communal Life

In his apostolic exhortation *Pastores Dabo Vobis* (*I Will Give You Shepherds*, 1992), John Paul II speaks of the place of chastity in the life of a celibate person, underlining the importance of love, communion, and the gift of self: "In virginity and celibacy, chastity retains its original meaning, that is, of human sexuality lived as a genuine sign of and precious service to the love of communion and gift of self to others."[3]

Expanding on this notion, he goes on to say that formation in sexuality for the celibate person "should be truly and fully personal and therefore should present chastity in a manner that shows appreciation and love for it as a virtue that develops a person's authentic maturity and makes him or her capable of respecting and fostering the 'nuptial meaning' of the body'" (*PDV* 44).

For a consecrated man living in common with others, this "communion" expresses itself first of all in his love for his brothers. We cannot live without giving and receiving love and friendship. While it is important to *state* the centrality of communion and love in celibate relationships, it is equally imperative to *foster* sound, healthy, and godly relationships in a concrete expression of common life. Given the profound challenges of living chaste celibacy in our time, what does this love and friendship in a real community look like on the ground? And how can the celibate man cultivate healthy relationships of love and friendship that both express and preserve his vocation?

All of us come to consecrated life with wounds, some much more than others. No one is without need of transformation. In my judgment, the crucial *foundational* ingredient for achieving healthy relationships—in this case, between brothers—is an environment and culture that is *already* godly and humanly healthy, into which a man can be welcomed. By this I mean a culture that is genuinely

God centered and that allows for and encourages free, authentic, manly relationships between the brothers to develop.

No human relational grouping (family or celibate community) is perfect, but there are such things as healthy (and unhealthy) communities. What are the marks of a healthy, godly community of men in which the members can grow toward sexual integrity and peace? The founders by their own example play a fundamental role in creating a healthy, godly environment that shapes the ongoing life of the community. The presence of confident, grounded men living in genuine friendship with each other—both within leadership and crisscrossing the community—provides ties that unite as well as the *space* for others to enter and find a place. Friendships cannot revolve around one person as the hub of relational life; this inevitably fosters the wrong kind of dependence. Instead, a healthy community, in which celibate love and friendship flourish, provides a network of relationships, each with its own quality, where each member can find his place and grow.

In a vibrant, flourishing community, there is likely to be profound unity in aims and convictions, but at the same time a great diversity of gifts and personalities that are united around a common way of life. This paradox—profound unity with great diversity of personality—expresses something important about a community of consecrated men. If the community is working well, it will allow the various individuals to find their own place and to offer themselves fully to God and to others in freedom. All this is conducive to, and crucial for, the fruit of an integrated, mature sexuality in the members.

Another mark of a healthy community is the experience of genuine friendship and affection without the grip of jealousy. As it is often observed, true and mature friendship is not *jealous*; it does not seek to bind someone exclusively and keep him from others. Unlike erotic love, which is rightfully exclusive between spouses, friendships in community ought to be warm and affectionate but genuinely open to others. As Thomas Dubay confirms, special friendships within community are "non-exclusive, non-possessive. Each friend is pleased that the other has other close relationships."[4]

In the section of our rule of life on brotherly love, we underline the joy that we ought to find in relationships with our brothers, but we also say that these relationships should be generous and open. In particular, we aim to avoid possessiveness, exclusiveness, and anxiousness to please another. In fact, the ability to enter into such joyful relationships freely *without possessiveness* is one important sign of a vocation to consecrated life. For a consecrated man, the ability to give himself personally to others freely and affectionately but without exclusivity is crucial for advancing toward a healthy and sound sexuality. The man who is overzealous—or who is incapable of forming genuine friendships freely because of fear, insecurity, or some past wound—may not be well suited to community life. Through prayer and counsel, over time he may break through and experience the ability to give of himself to others freely. But without this trait being established and demonstrated, it is best for such a man not to make a permanent commitment to the community.

A third mark of healthy relationships and communal life—a trait difficult to describe well—is a spirit of joy that often expresses itself in humor. Christ, of course, calls us to be serious and sober in following him, living with purpose and intention. Good humor doesn't undermine this serious purpose but prevents us from taking ourselves and our own weaknesses too seriously.

Humor must always be tempered with gentleness—the scriptures make clear that we are to build one another up and to honor one another in daily life. When humor—especially directed at pointing out the foibles of others—becomes the *dominant* mode of conversation in a community, then something has gone wrong and must be brought back into balance. But humor has its place, and one sign of a healthy community—and healthy relationships among brothers—is the presence of a joyful good humor operating within genuine and affectionate friendships.

Much more could be said about the importance of healthy friendships for growing in personal sexuality integrity, but I want to add here that consecrated men can and should have healthy relationships with families, including with women and children. The primary relationships that support a consecrated life are with one's own brothers, but there is an important place for a wider network of relationships and friendships that give both joy and balance to life.

Raniero Cantalamessa offers insight into the positive interaction that can occur between families and celibate men and women: "How useful it is that there should be a healthy integration of charisms in the Christian community, whereby married people and celibates do not live in strict separation from one another, but in such a way that they can help and encourage one another to grow."[5]

These relationships can take time to develop, and may require periodic adjustments as imbalances arise, by one party being either too diffident or too intimate. Learning how to enter into such relationships—each one with its own special qualities—is an important part of giving of oneself freely and appropriately, in accordance with a commitment to celibate chastity. People from married and celibate vocations have much to offer each other on their common pilgrimage. Learning and relearning how to give of oneself appropriately within various relationships is part of growing into a full and healthy sexual integrity.

3. Openness and Accountability

If a consecrated man has not set his heart on purity, then there is little hope that he will remain faithful to his commitments. If he harbors secret desires at odds with the life he has chosen to live, deep conflicts will emerge. An essential condition, then, for a consecrated man to live a life of sexual integrity is a commitment *to seek purity of heart and body* on the one hand, and on the other a commitment to *specific practices* that help him to live purely. This means both attaching himself to the positive steps and committing himself to avoid those things that war against a chaste, consecrated life.

We must be prepared to *fight* for purity in our lives, and this means learning how to struggle—to do battle—for the good. The idea of fighting, of struggling, and of doing battle is not popular today. But scripture is filled with language and images of doing battle for the good, and the spiritual classics over the ages under-line the supreme importance of learning to do battle. There's a good reason why the *Catechism of the Catholic Church* titles the sub-section after "Purification of the Heart" as "The Battle for Purity" (CCC 2520).

One important ingredient in this struggle for purity is finding a place to speak openly and honestly about challenges related to sexual purity, either in one-to-one conversation or in a small group.[6] Learning how to "live in the light" in an open, modest way is a crucial part of formation and growth toward sexual maturity. Here, each consecrated community will have its own special prac-tices and vehicles. In my experience, the practice of accountabil-ity—of living in the light—cannot normally be handled well by the confessional *alone*. In fact, some men can misuse the Sacrament of Reconciliation by using it as a place to *hide* their sins and failures from notice by anyone else, imagining that they are truly living in the light. A man normally needs a further context—and often more than one—in which to gain help, speak honestly of his challenges, and be held accountable by his brothers for living faithfully.

What I wish to speak to, then, are elements that could be part of any care system for a consecrated man. The immense failures of celibate men that have been brought to light only underline how important this aspect of care is for growth toward a mature, inte-grated sexuality. In the recent past, in both the Christian commu-nity and in the wider society, there were protections that helped people keep faithful to their commitments; today these external helps are largely absent.

And so, as Cantalamessa points out, "the defense of one's chastity is now for the most part in the hands of the individual, and it cannot rest on anything other than strong personal con-victions, acquired precisely with God in prayer in His Word."[7] The choice to intentionally surround oneself with support and accountability is part of how we need to actively cultivate purity and a healthy expression of our sexuality. It should be said that when speaking about matters of our sexual history, we don't normally divulge details and names. We share in a way that makes clear what the area is, but we naturally limit the information we give about specifics.

What kinds of issues are we concerned with that are helpful to bring into the light? First of all, we are concerned with actual sexual encounters in the past (or possibly even in the present) with other people. A man needs to come to grips with these, gain a basic understanding of them, repent of them, and receive prayer for healing from any impact those sexual encounters may have had.[8] Beyond these, the most common areas to work through are pornography, masturbation, and sexual fantasy.

The first of these, pornography, has truly become a plague in our day, such that almost every young man has to overcome some level of addiction to online pornography. Gaining help with this and adopting strategies for staying clear over time are crucial steps toward sexual purity and peace. Likewise, gaining freedom from masturbation and growing in mastery over sexual fantasy are critical for the goal of mature, sexual integrity. Why is this so? Because sexual integrity includes health, wholeness, peace, and righteousness in our sexuality. It is only when we come to see our sexuality and our bodies—and those of others—in the light of God's good, creative plan that we can proceed toward mature sexual wholeness.

A key part of sexual purity is purity *of mind*, and this must come from God and his Word. As in all other areas, we are called to be "transformed by the renewal of [our] mind" (Rom 12:2) regarding our sexuality, seeing ourselves and others with the mind and the "eye" of God himself. According to Cantalamessa, "a healthy *knowledge* and *acceptance* of the sexual component of our life is also a valuable aid to living our charism peacefully. . . . We must learn how to look at the opposite sex, at procreation, and at children, with pure eyes, in short, with the eyes like those of Jesus."[9]

In summary, every man will need help in this area—primarily from God but certainly as well from his brothers in Christ. It is a sign of mature freedom when a man can speak directly about sexual challenges that he has faced in the past and that he faces in the present, and gain the help and encouragement from others to press on and not give up. Most men experience the same (or similar) challenges in their sexuality, and yet most men naturally do not want to speak about these challenges! The result is that they remain hidden and unattended, and block the path to mature sexual health and peace. But when men find a context in which they can speak of sexual issues openly and yet with modesty, knowing that what they say will be held in confidence, healing and transformation are much more likely to occur.

Cultivating Chastity and Modesty

If we aim for a life of purity and integrity in which we are poised to give ourselves to God fully and to serve others gladly in love, then the virtues of chastity and modesty must be in attendance. These are not popular virtues today. They tend to be mocked and derided, even by Christians, as something from a Victorian past needing to be jettisoned. But the goal is not to become Victorian in our manners and speech; it is to live a life of rightly ordered and expressed sexuality that enables us to love God and others freely and well.

The description of chastity has undergone notable modifications in the past century. A much-beloved classic text of ascetical theology, *The Spiritual Life* by Adolphe Tanquerey, asserts that "the aim of chastity is to check whatever is inordinate in voluptuous pleasures."[10] Tanquerey emphasizes both the centrality and the fragility of this virtue: "Chastity is a frail and delicate virtue that cannot be preserved unless it be protected by other virtues. It is, as it were, a citadel that requires for its defense the raising of outward ramparts."[11]

Tanquerey's treatment of chastity is full of the language of duty, of mortification, and of flight from things that war against chastity. There is a great deal of wisdom in this older account: it is very realistic and pulls no punches; it is serious and calls readers to apply themselves. But it is also (I would say) *severe* in its treatment of the entire area. There is something just a bit grim in how it depicts the struggle and the fight.

The *Catechism of the Catholic Church* provides a rather different treatment of chastity. Many of the principles and truths from Tanquerey are present, so there is genuine continuity, and yet it also breathes the air of personalism, of the exercise of freedom in seeking the good. It places chastity in a wider context than just lustful desire, as the following selections reveal:

> Chastity means the successful integration of sexuality within the person and thus the inner unity of man in his bodily and spiritual being. (2337)
>
> The chaste person maintains the integrity of the powers of life and love placed in him. This integrity ensures the unity of the person; it is opposed to any behavior that would impair it. It tolerates neither a double life nor duplicity in speech. (2338)

On this broader account, it is chastity that brings about the integration—the internal unity—of a person, of body and soul in Christ. It brings about a fruitful balance of powers ordered to love and won't allow practices or habits that assault this order of unity and love. One of my favorite lines from the *Catechism* speaks about the inner self-mastery that chastity brings: "Chastity includes an *apprenticeship in self-mastery* which is a training in human freedom" (CCC 2239, emphasis in original). Who does not desire this?

The *Catechism*, in the end, does not soft-pedal chastity. It offers firm and concrete markers by which chastity must be obtained. Like Tanquerey, the *Catechism* affirms that the path to chastity is arduous; self-mastery "is a *long and exacting work*" that "presupposes renewed effort at all stages of life" (CCC 2342, emphasis in original). It outlines in great detail the things that offend against chastity, and shows how they can be overcome (see CCC, 2351–2356). And importantly, the *Catechism* describes the essential link between chastity and godly friendship:

The virtue of chastity blossoms in *friendship*. It shows the disciple how to follow and imitate him who has chosen us as his friends, who has given himself totally to us and allows us to participate in his divine estate. . . .

Chastity is expressed notably in *friendship with one's neighbor*. Whether it develops between persons of the same or opposite sex, friendship represents a great good for all. It leads to spiritual communion. (CCC, 2347, emphasis in the original)

For the consecrated man, chastity requires at its core a clear line of vision: clear sight and clear thinking. We have to do our best to get rid of illusions about ourselves; to name things as they are. Having a confidant, a mentor, or a "band of brothers" can be immensely helpful here. A man needs to not only know himself but also become master of the process that leads toward purity, understanding the concrete pathways by which he can walk in faithfulness. Given the challenge of gaining the virtue of chastity in its fullness, we require a large store of patience and forgiveness, for ourselves and for others.

Finally, we ought to pursue an understanding of chastity that puts the emphasis on others. Even as we take the hard, demanding steps required to achieve this virtue, our main focus should not be upon ourselves but rather on God and the good of others. One of the most important steps on the path to sexual integrity is to be concerned primarily for the well-being and flourishing of others. Where does the virtue of modesty make its contribution? The *Catechism* again offers an excellent, concise description of how modesty contributes to mature sexuality:

Modesty protects the intimate center of the person. It means refusing to unveil what should remain hidden. It is ordered to chastity to whose sensitivity it bears witness. It guides how one looks at others and behaves toward them in conformity with the dignity of persons and their solidarity. (CCC 2521)

More generally, "modesty protects the mystery of persons and their love" (CCC 2522). Quite tellingly, modesty not only serves the individual by guarding a God-given treasure within but also furnishes a "relational" service by preserving the love of individuals. Though the practices of modesty will differ from culture to culture, modesty exists everywhere as a "spiritual dignity" proper to human beings (CCC 2524).

Consecrated brothers who live together must strike a balance between being "natural" (feeling at home) and at the same time preserving modesty and guarding chastity in the way we relate to each other and to our bodies. When the common aim is to live out a chaste masculine sexuality, good practices will normally follow. But as the long wisdom from the tradition teaches, we ought to be on our guard and not be naïve about what can go wrong. A community must always be actively building up its way of life through healthy and godly practices and renew its commitment to them, or else it will slowly slip its moorings and proceed down the road to unfaithfulness, wondering how it has drifted this far from its original purpose.

Seeking Compensations and Substitutes

Lifelong celibacy requires serious renunciation, and this comes with a cost. Knowing and experiencing the "pinch" of that cost is part of what keeps a celibate man sharp and focused on first things. At the start, when zeal is running high, this cost is gladly paid and met, and the joys and satisfactions of prayer or of fruitful apostolic labor seem to more than compensate for what has been given up.

But over time, especially as prayer patterns become dryer and relationships run aground upon mutual weaknesses and mission seems less compelling, the temptation to seek substitutes and compensations will arise. The same is true for married people—each vocation has its temptation to seek compensations outside of the vocation itself. It is important to recognize this category of temptation because normally a man falls prey to these compensations without realizing what is happening.

It should be obvious that seeking sexual gratification from others, male or female, is not only gravely sinful but a very poor substitute for the great good of marriage that a consecrated man has forgone. But what I am addressing here are the kinds of substitutes and compensations that don't obviously appear as being unfaithful to the call. As Thomas Dubay notes, "Perhaps the most subtle danger for men and women who have given up the values of married love, private property, and the self-disposition of their persons is the gradual, almost imperceptible drift into compensation seeking."[12]

One very common substitution occurs when we seek out and cultivate special relationships from which we receive the kind of personal encouragement and intimacy appropriate to marriage. We fool ourselves and insist that these relationships are fine because nothing overtly sexual is occurring. But having the kind of relationship with another that approximates the intimacy of marriage is a form of unfaithfulness to one's consecrated call. These relationships should be distinguished from healthy and warm friendships with men and women, which are a very good thing for a consecrated man to cultivate.

How do we tell the difference? First, a warning light should go off when we are spending a lot of time with one person, one-on-one, sharing intimate details of life. This is much more than a good friendship; it is supplying a kind of marital emotional intimacy. Second, the wrong kind of friendships tend to show signs of jealousy—of wanting someone for ourselves. And third, they tend to be focused on what "I" need from the relationship, rather than being oriented to giving to others in the midst of affectionate friendships.

To cultivate healthy friendships while working to keep them from becoming inappropriate relationships requires real effort. Those nearest to us can often see signs of this before we do and can advise us about a relationship that may be taking an inappropriate turn. Equally common is the tendency to compensate for loneliness or emotional need by taking refuge in some kind of pleasurable activity that satisfies and helps to bracket out whatever pain or trial we are experiencing. Thus, we see the pattern of celibate men becoming gourmet cooks, or masters of mixed drinks, or world travelers, or master gardeners, or expert theatergoers. Now all of these activities can be beneficial within limits. But there is a clear temptation for a celibate man—often because he has more time and freedom on his hands—to pursue these activities in an intemperate way, in a way not fitting to his call and vocation.

In this sense, these activities then become competitors and begin to block spiritual growth. How do substitutes and compensations affect growth in sexual integrity? A consecrated man must reach full *human* maturity if he is to achieve sexual integrity. When we give ourselves over to substitutes—to things that fill our life and make them more palatable—we are falling short of this maturity. We are acting more as adolescents than mature adults, and in fact for some men the celibate context can impede growth into full human maturity. A consecrated man will not reach sexual integrity by hiding out in special relationships or distracting activities but only by fully and honestly embracing the cost of his consecration, offering it to God, and finding as the fruit of this offering a true, mature freedom to love others.

Balancing Life: Prayer, Community, Service

Growth into full maturity—and mature sexual integrity—involves finding a way to join together and harmonize *prayer*, *life in community*, and *one's apostolic work*. Again, the challenge here is one faced by all Christians, married and celibate. But for a consecrated man there are certain blessings and challenges (advantages and disadvantages) that require special strategies.

One advantage possessed by the consecrated man is his rule of life. This ought to provide him a great deal of help in achieving balance and order, yet each man needs to constantly work this out in his own circumstances. Because a consecrated man has a more open schedule (he has no commitment to a wife and children that naturally call for his attention), he can more easily lean into imbalances, the most common one being the tendency to overwork.

One sign of this imbalance is physical and mental strain, often the result of working constantly and not finding the right kind of rest, recreation, and communal support. Another sign is a restlessness of the soul that is seeking something it does not have in hand. Often it is looking for substitutes and compensations that make it more difficult to live well and faithfully. In both of these instances, a man's sexual and relational integrity may be adversely affected. The remedy usually involves a recommitment to prayer—including personal prayer—and to the community, especially individual relationships. In short, what is needed is a reinvestment in the love of God and neighbor that will make apostolic work fruitful and life-giving.

Conclusion

The path to sexual integrity—that is, to wholeness, peace, righteousness, purity, and freedom in the sexual sphere of life—possesses the same essential features for married and celibate and for men and women. But the special qualities that mark the path for each kind of vocation, and the distinctive experiences of men and women, justify attention to the particular contexts and strategies that pertain to each state in life. I have attempted to identify the typical narrative structure that a man will follow as a disciple of Christ on the path to consecrated life, and to describe the *relationships, virtues,* and *practices*—and most especially *the call and grace of God*—that provide the wider context for his growth into sexual integrity.

It is fitting to close with a word that turns our attention to the Lord God in thanksgiving. To be called and to be set aside for Christ is a great privilege, not something that we can deserve and certainly not something we can carry out by our own power. It is by the call and ongoing grace of God that we set out and continue on this path, and it is through praise and thanksgiving that we keep our feet solidly underneath us and so are enabled to press on.

> How can I repay the Lord
> for all the great good done for me?
> I will raise the cup of salvation

> and call on the name of the LORD.
> I will offer a sacrifice of praise
>   and call on the name of the LORD.
> I will pay my vows to the LORD
>   in the presence of all his people. . . .
> In the courts of the house of the LORD,
>   in your midst, O Jerusalem. (Ps 116:12–14, 19)

Questions for Reflection

1. Are there distinctive qualities that mark the path toward mature sexual integrity for a consecrated man? If yes, what are the main qualities, and how do they apply to my situation?

2. Why is it important to draw models primarily from God's purposeful design rather than from notions current in popular culture? What are the main sources from which I derive my vision of what my sexuality should look like?

3. God has given us great dignity in offering us the opportunity to cooperate with his call in our lives and to choose to live for him (if called) as a celibate man. How have you experienced this call and responded in your life? What insights can you gain by looking back (or forward) to the dignity of electing a celibate vocation?

4. Which of the elements of a fruitful consecrated life spoke to you most powerfully? In which areas are you especially strong? Is there an area of weakness and limitation? What are some steps you might take to grow in this element of consecrated life?

CHAPTER 8

LOVE AND INTIMACY AS A RELIGIOUS SISTER

SARA FAIRBANKS, O.P.

In this poignant, inspiring chapter, Sr. Sara Fairbanks describes her journey into the discovery of what it means to be a religious sister whose love for God and others led to a commitment to celibacy, which involved a process of transformation. This transformation occurred by working through childhood wounds to self-acceptance, to the discovery of what it means to be a contemplative in action, a religious dedicated to the adventures of ministerial life. In the process she became convicted that "falling in love and staying in love with God and all that God loves is at the heart of healthy, integrated sexuality."

In 1985, at the age of twenty-nine, I joined the Dominican Sisters of Adrian, Michigan. God's gift of self—"I am with you always"—had inspired within me a deep desire to reciprocate with a gift of my own self, given freely and completely.

Before I could do this, however, I felt the need to address some strong challenges around religious celibacy: *Does living the vow of celibacy mean giving up my sexuality? Will celibacy stunt my development toward mature adulthood? Isn't this kind of commitment out of step with the times?* By engaging these challenges with friends and loved ones, I clarified in my own heart the compelling reasons that motivated me to commit wholeheartedly to God in a way that excluded any other primary commitments, including marriage and family.

Especially in the years leading up to my entering religious life, my experience of God's love had been so direct, powerful, and life changing, I desired to proclaim with my life the profound truth that God alone satisfies the deepest longings of the human heart. I was drawn to the Dominican charism because this life provided me the freedom to live a life of contemplation in action. Not only did I have the contemplative time and space to develop my relationship with God, but I was also totally available for the adventures of a ministerial life shared in common with my Dominican sisters.

While it is true that celibacy clearly requires abstinence from genital sexual activity, and that I will never love and be loved as wife and mother, my vows did not entail renouncing my sexuality. Rather, my vow of celibacy opened the door to a lifelong process of transformation that leads to self-acceptance and healthy, life-giving intimacy with God, with other people, and with all of creation.

Understanding Sexuality

In their book *Tender Fires: The Spiritual Promise of Sexuality*, psychologists Fran Ferder and John Heagle explain how Western culture came to understand sexuality primarily as genital behavior. They assert that, until recently, most religious traditions taught that the primary purpose of sexuality is its biological function, as a necessary means to propagate the human race.

It was only after our understanding of sexual intimacy evolved to include a second, equally important unitive goal (strengthening the mutual love of the couple) that religious traditions began to recognize the emotional, psychic, and spiritual dimensions of sexuality.[1] This development represented an important first step, but this understanding of the meaning and purpose of sexuality was still limited primarily to marriage. Our religious tradition today, however, recognizes a more expansive way of envisioning sexuality as energy for relationships. The *Catechism of the Catholic Church* teaches that sexuality is "the aptitude for forming bonds of communion with others" (2332).

Sexuality is a complex concept that most basically refers to our love energy, the yearning for intimacy and connection that emerges in our lives even before we are born. Ferder and Heagle refer to sexuality as "the spiritual, emotional, physical, psychological, social and cultural aspects of relating to one another as embodied male and female persons."[2]

Sexuality is the energy for interpersonal connection that is expressed in a variety of ways through faithful couples, loving families, nurturing friendships, caring communities, and dynamic work environments. As Ferder and Heagle assert, "We are all sexual—all the time. Unlike our genital feelings, our sexuality does not wax and wane—it is always with us."[3] Psychologists also recognize that "having sex" in this over-sexed culture of internet pornography and casual hookups can represent a fear of intimacy, an escape from authentic and intimate sexuality.

Growing in Love as a Celibate Woman

As a celibate lover, I need to share intimacy in life-giving ways as much as a married person does. Since God is at the heart of my love life, and loving God is united to loving neighbor as myself, my sexuality and spirituality go hand in hand. My spirituality grounds, guides, and integrates my sexual energies for relationship in the lifelong process of becoming a happy and mature adult.

Getting my basic needs met in self-affirming ways required developing a multiplicity of personal skills, from communication skills that foster healthy self-esteem, self-nurturance, and assertiveness, to skills for prayer and intimacy with God, to interpersonal skills for trust and compassion, as well as a number of skills for professional competence and personal freedom.

My relational life is also rooted in my commitment to my religious community of Dominican sisters with whom I live and share faith and mission. Sharing our material resources, we work to establish the kind of community life that will support and strengthen our ability to spread the Gospel and to be in solidarity and service to those who are poor and most vulnerable in our world.

I will first discuss celibate sexuality through the lens of my own vocation story in order to illustrate what it means to me to live healthy, integrated sexuality as a Dominican sister. Then, I will explore one central practice that I have found essential in developing lifelong intimacy with God, myself, and others that is so necessary for living healthy, integrated sexuality.

Falling in Love with God

My story begins in 1956, in a small town cradled in the mapled mountains of Vermont. Sandy, my twin sister, was born one hour ahead of me, which makes me the youngest of five children. (Another sister and two brothers preceded us.) I am especially close to Sandy, who has been a loving companion throughout my life. My mother was a housewife, and my father a mailman. My dad also ran the family vegetable business, in which we all worked.

My dad, who had no religious upbringing, converted to Catholicism to marry my mom, who was a first-generation Polish-Russian immigrant. Our whole family went to church every Sunday. There was no Catholic school in town, so we attended weekly catechism classes with the sisters, which I enjoyed. Because my dad loved athletics, I played many backyard sports with my sister and brothers. I also played team sports with my classmates. Not being very athletic, I enjoyed the social dimension of the games the most.

In high school, my social life revolved around music. Most of my friends were in the band, so I taught myself to play my brother's old trumpet and joined the concert band. I also played in the marching band, pep band, pit band for school plays, and town band. In my junior year, our concert band won the opportunity to participate in an international music festival in Vienna, Austria. Music enriched my life and provided me with a wonderful network of friends. In these years, I took my first tentative steps dating boys, but no serious relationships developed.

In the fall of 1974, I left home to attend a small Presbyterian women's college in Pennsylvania. The hardest part of leaving home was saying good-bye to my sister Sandy when we parted ways for the first time to go to different colleges. In my newfound freedom I quit going to church, although I did want a relationship with God.

Like any college student, I was anxious about succeeding in school, making a career for myself, building friendships, and finding a loving husband. I was a European history major. In my junior year, my academic adviser directed me to take a course on the Protestant Reformation through the religion department because that particular split in Christendom had powerful political ramifications for all of Europe.

So quite unexpectedly, I ended up taking my first college religion class. During the course, our professor explained that a key theme of the Protestant reform was the right of every Christian to read the Bible in his or her own language. He concluded his lecture with this summons: "I challenge each one of you here to pick up the Bible and read one of the gospels all the way through."

One night I decided to take up his challenge. I didn't own a Bible, so I borrowed one from a Protestant friend and opened to the Gospel of Matthew. When I got to the Sermon on the Mount, and read the passage where Jesus says, "Ask and it will be given to you; seek and you will find; knock and the door will be opened to you" (Mt 7:7), I sensed for the first time the personal presence of God with me, speaking these words directly to my heart. These words awakened me to a divine love that I had never known before, a love unsurpassed.

Ask and it will be given to you. What openhanded, unconditional love! It was not, "Get good grades, and I will love you," or "Do what I say, and I will love you." Rather, I experienced God as an awesome yet incredibly humble and alluring presence.

Knock and the door will be opened to you. The Creator of the universe was granting me easy access and inviting me to come close. I sensed I was sitting in God's presence, and felt for the first time new eyes beholding me in love. I was in tears and full of joy! This exercise of reading scripture proved to be more than I expected. I realized that night that God's love was real, and my life was changed forever. I was on a high—"walking on sunshine," as the Katrina and the Waves song goes—for weeks. And it felt good.

I returned to church, eager to find a way to sustain this personal encounter with God, to keep this relationship going. I had so many questions: *How do I share my daily life with Holy Mystery? When I talk to God, should I expect to hear God speaking back to me? Am I going to hear a voice from the clouds?* I had so many questions, and wasn't sure where to find the answers.

A few weeks later I returned home to Vermont and resumed my summer job as a waitress. I began to read *The Diary of Anne Frank.* I was completely taken up with this young woman's story! I was impressed with her self-esteem and love of life even though she was hiding in an attic with her family to escape the Nazis. She talks about her problems with her mother, her new boyfriend, everything that is going on. Like Anne, I wanted to be the kind of person who could experience the joy of living, no matter how difficult the circumstances. I thought, *Maybe if I keep a journal, I will become more like her.*

You may recall that Anne titled her journal "Kitty" and began every entry as she would a letter, "Dear Kitty." "Kitty" became her friend and confidante. I found myself wondering, If I were to write a journal, what name would I give it? Whom do I want to be my friend and confidante? I wanted this kind of relationship with God, so I began my journal, "Dear God," and I started to write down everything that was going on in my life. In the middle of this exercise, however, I thought, *This is really silly! My life is not important to God. My little, ordinary, day-to-day activities are hardly interesting to God. This kind of relationship with God is just not possible.* I finished the letter anyway and signed it, "Love, Sara."

That weekend I went to Sunday liturgy at our parish church. To my surprise, the visiting priest's homily was in the form of a letter from God, addressing all of us with love. I sat there in awe. My letter to God had been answered! I was in tears. The message I received was "Sara, don't quit on me now; we are just getting started." Whether we are aware of it or not, God is a pure, loving Presence, who values us and takes delight in our company. With unthinkable humility, God seeks a relationship with us, even more than we seek a relationship with God.

Journeying toward Sexual and Spiritual Maturity

Fast forward to 1979. I moved to Bryn Mawr College to pursue a master's degree in history. During my three years of study there, I developed a close circle of female friends with whom I could talk and share life. A popular book circulating among us, *Our Bodies, Ourselves: A Book by and for Women,* helped me to learn more about genital sexuality, my body, and the orgasmic pleasures of my female anatomy. It was also at this time that I began dating different men, and fell in and out of love a few times, learning the hard way the meaning of infatuation. I was aware of my feelings of sexual arousal and enjoyed some physical intimacies with my boyfriends, though I had decided that I wanted to wait until marriage before having sexual intercourse. I wanted my sexual expressions to reflect the truth of our relationship and the level of commitment we had for each other.

During this time, I continued to cultivate my spiritual life through reading scripture and prayer. I regularly took books out of the library on the saints and mystics. I discovered Catherine of Siena, who called God "a gentle lover," even a "mad lover"—"a fire that takes away the chill in my heart."[4] I read Francis of Assisi, Francis de Sales, Meister Eckhart, and many others who bedazzled me. "If you truly have God and only God, nothing could disturb you," says Eckhart.[5] Soon I found Teresa of Avila and read her *Autobiography* and *The Interior Castle*. Even though much of what she said seemed exotic and way beyond my experience—spiritual betrothal, exquisite woundings of the soul, raptures, locutions, visions, all culminating in marriage to God—I was awed by the witness of her spiritual experience of God's personal relationship of intimacy with her and how that experience deepened her love of herself and others.

In *The Interior Castle*, she writes: "It came to my mind . . . that we consider our soul to be like a castle made entirely out of a diamond or of very clear crystal, in which there are many rooms. . . . Sisters, we realize that the soul of the just person is nothing else but a paradise where Christ says He finds His delight."[6] Her voice, in concert with the others, was encouraging me to awaken to my own inner beauty where God dwells.

As I slowly developed my interior life, I began to see how negative dynamics in my relationships were stirring up feelings and situations reminiscent of childhood. I became acutely aware of my need to do some grief work over my difficult relationships with my mother and father.

Fortuitously, I discovered Dennis and Matthew Linn's book, *Healing Life's Hurts*. With the help of their guided meditation and journaling process using scripture, I moved through the normal stages of healing memories: denial, anger, bargaining, depression, and acceptance. I learned to open up to myself, to go deep down inside my world, underneath, and to share my painful childhood memories with God. Through this intense grief work, I experienced God's attentive and nurturing love.

As I continued to converse with God, I began to let go of my childhood image of God that looked a lot like my relationship with my troubled parents. I also grew in self-acceptance and personal integration. This was a lengthy process that spanned several years. I also learned better communication skills in dealing with conflict, which I practiced with my parents to a great advantage. At the same time, I sought short-term therapeutic counseling to help me work through some of these family dynamics. This inner work taught me to be more self-reliant and self-compassionate in attending to my feelings, to lower my expectations about how others will meet my relational needs, to feel empathy and forgiveness toward my parents, and to establish healthier boundaries in my relational life.

This foundational inner work is the bedrock of authentic sexuality. It was only the beginning of lifelong work that became easier as I continued to develop self-esteem and new relational skills along the way. In an "O, happy fault" kind of way, this painful grief work profoundly strengthened my trust and love bond with God. Through this form of scripture-based prayer, I could share with Jesus what matters most to me and hear his liberating response in return. In many ways this was an Exodus experience where God gradually led me out of the bondage of fear, anger, shame, and grief into the promised land of self-renewal and self-gift. God wipes away every tear from our eyes and makes all things new.

Discovering My Vocation

In my last year at Bryn Mawr, I began to sneak off campus to daily Mass. I also taught Sunday school at my local parish with the Sisters of Mercy. In my role as a catechist, I agreed to attend a catechetical conference where the keynote speaker was a Franciscan priest who talked about his ministry with homeless, runaway teenagers through Covenant House, located in New York's Time Square. At the end of his presentation, he said: "I challenge anyone here in the audience to give a year of your life and come live with me in community, do childcare with the homeless teenagers, and pray three hours a day. I will give you room and board, and $12 per week."

When I heard this invitation, my heart lit up. I was thrilled about this opportunity for prayer, community life, and ministry, without having to worry about taking religious vows. A year later, in 1982, I joined the Covenant House community along with seventy other men and women, mostly in our mid-twenties. We could date but were committed to chaste love.

As I worked with the teenage mothers and their babies, I felt thankful and honored to be called by Jesus to partner with him in this mission. These young mothers were children themselves, often running from abusive family situations, out of school, unemployed, and totally unprepared to take on the responsibilities of parenthood. In all their vulnerability, I saw their love and courage to keep fighting for a better life for themselves and their children. I also got a glimpse at the breadth and depth of God's unconditional love for all humanity, especially the last and the least. God is a "mad lover," who cares about everybody. At the end of my first year, I recommitted for another two, and went to Fort Lauderdale, Florida, with two other community members to open a new Covenant House.

At this point I realized that I felt drawn to religious life, and sought a spiritual director to help me discern what God was asking of me. My experience of Covenant House was very telling. I thrived on the three hours of prayer a day, the community life, and the ministry. I had never been happier. And yet I had been dating a young man while I was working there. So the question was, Could I forgo the intimacy of married life and having a family? As I wrestled with this in prayer, I heard God saying, "I will love you just as much no matter what you choose. What do you really desire to do with your life?"

God desires what we most deeply desire. I really wanted and needed the contemplative time and space for a single-hearted pursuit of my relationship with God. God's loving companionship met the deepest desires of my heart. Significant time with God every morning was the best and most renewing part of my day. I experienced celibacy not as a torturous struggle, but as a gift of the Holy Spirit affirming my desire for religious life. I had always enjoyed a circle of close men and women friends, and while motherhood had a certain appeal, I did not sense a strong call to be a mother. I had experienced God's loving presence at the core of my being, and I wanted to live into that presence in ever-deeper ways through my ministry and my community life.

I worked through this process of discernment with my spiritual director, Sr. Mary Mullins, whom I later learned had been for many years the novice director for the Dominican Sisters of Adrian. As she got to know me, she began to give me books on St. Dominic and Catherine of Siena, as well as the Adrian Dominican Constitution. I began to spend time with different communities of her sisters so we could share our faith experiences as well as understandings of religious life.

Because choosing a compatible community is so important, Mary encouraged me to consider other religious congregations, like the Sisters of Mercy and the Franciscans, as well as other Dominican congregations, to find the right fit. After a year of exploring the unique charisms of a variety of congregations, I visited the motherhouse in Adrian, Michigan, and began the arduous application process. Once I entered, I had three years of theological and religious formation. Upon completion, I mutually discerned with my congregation to make first vows; four years later, in 1993, I made my final vows.

Falling in love with God brought me to a most unexpected and radical decision to become a Dominican sister, having encountered in a deeply personal way the power of God's love to shape our lives through our everyday circumstances and activities. This passage resonated with me in a unique way:

> Nothing is more practical than finding God, that is, than falling in love in quite an absolute, final way. What you are in love with, what seizes your imagination, will affect everything. It will decide what will get you out of bed in the morning, what you will do with your evenings, how you will spend your weekends, what you read, whom you know, what breaks your heart, and what amazes you with joy and gratitude. Fall in love, stay in love—and it will decide everything.[7]

Falling in love and staying in love with God and all that God loves is at the heart of healthy, integrated sexuality. Perhaps the single most crucial skill for promoting lifelong intimacy with God, self, and others is attending to emotional wounds—a skill for sexual integrity that I will now discuss further.

Staying in Love

Staying in love with God, self, and others requires deep mutual attentiveness, unconditional love, and the courageous sharing of our emotional wounds. In their classic book, *The Practice of Spiritual Direction*, William A. Barry and William J. Connolly astutely point out that "as life affects us, God affects us, as we react to life, we react to God."[8]

We may react positively with awe, thanksgiving, and joyful acceptance of God and the world God has made. Alternatively, we may feel fear, devastating grief, anger, or shame at what is happening to us in God's world. Or we may have mixed reviews; we are happy with some aspects of our life, while discouraged and depressed by others. Often these reactions are buried deep beneath the surface of our consciousness and motivate us in hidden but powerful ways.

Coping with Past Grief and Loss

In his book *How to Be an Adult: A Handbook on Psychological and Spiritual Integration*, David Richo asserts that most people step into adulthood with conscious and unconscious psychic wounds accrued in childhood. "If the traumas of childhood go untreated, they will be repeated in the dramas of adulthood. Our problem is not that as children our needs were unmet, but that as adults they are still unmourned."[9]

Our memories of unconscious psychic wounds are triggered by current situations and relationships that generate strong adverse reactions. Our tendency is to focus on the upsetting situation and the other people involved. We get bound up in our instincts to fight or take flight that find expression in a variety of dysfunctional behaviors, wreaking havoc on our relationships.

Instead of reacting in this manner, I discovered a different approach laid out in two important books: Michael Brown's *The*

Presence Process: A Healing Journey into Present Moment Awareness, and David Richo's *When the Past Is the Present: Healing the Emotional Wounds That Sabotage Our Relationships*. Both authors wisely guide us to take our attention off the incident and focus on how we are feeling. We then track the feelings back to our childhood, where the hurt, betrayed, and grieving child is still within us, wanting to let go of her neediness and pain.

As we feel the pain and invite God's nurturing presence to be with us in all of our vulnerability, God, who is pure, unconditional love, shows us how to love ourselves unconditionally, gently encouraging us to connect with and treasure our child within. As our loving parent, God calls forth our own inner nurturing parent. With eyes of deep compassion, our inner parent helps the child within to let go, to realize that what we have lost is irretrievable and what we missed is irreplaceable. With this realization, we are finally free of the insatiable need to find it again in the people closest to us.

While grief work brings us face-to-face with our inner emptiness, it also reveals just as great a fullness; we discover a new love in the depths of our soul, where God makes a home.[10] In our relational lives, this self-parenting is the best condition for authentic intimacy to flourish. It trades childish dependency for mutually accountable interdependency that enables us to relate to the people with whom we live and work as equal adult partners.

As Richo states, "Only those who can take care of themselves are free from the two main obstacles to adult relating: being needy or care-taking others."[11] We stop playing the helpless, angry victim, blaming other people for our misfortunes. We drop our expectations that others are responsible for our happiness. Instead, we take responsibility for our feelings and behavior, communicating clearly our thoughts and feelings, learning to ask for what we want. We quit our controlling behavior and respect other people's boundaries. Likewise, we protect our health and well-being by limiting our time around negative people and environments. We cherish other people with our acceptance, affirmation, and appreciation, as well as our honest challenge. We enjoy the give-and-take of such unconditional love, honesty, and respect. We are capable of real commitment in good times and bad. In sum, we love one another as Christ has loved us (see John 13:34–35).

This kind of prayerful grief work also promotes self-esteem because it reveals our courage in facing the painful truths of our lives. Such heroic handling of sufferings also develops our capacity for unconditional love. In discovering the tender, yet invincible parent-child bond within, we experience integration, wholeness, and the peace only God can give. In this process, our self-God image is also transformed.

In my own experience of attending to emotional wounds, my image of self as an unworthy, problem child whom God graciously saves has evolved into the image of self as a healthy adult, meeting God as friend, as spouse, as highly favored daughter, as dedicated partner in mission. In light of God's self-gift of love, my heart is flooded with gratitude. I am freer and less dependent on the approval of others. I can give a modest yes to God's playful yet compelling question: "Are my eyes enough for you?" As I grow in self-love, I am more open and able to receive the gift of God's attention, affirmation, and life-giving presence. I am also more able to acknowledge that my life is a true gift to God. I can enjoy God's pleasure in my company and hear the humility and tenderness in God's "thank you for loving me." Staying in love with God is at the heart of my sexual integrity, and animates my personal, relational, and ministerial life.

Questions for Reflection

1. What has been your experience of falling in love with God? Staying in love with God?

2. What are some of the ways your relationship with God has influenced your relational life?

3. What is your attitude toward religious celibacy? Is it an option you would consider for yourself? Would you support such a choice for a family member or friend?

4. What are some ways you have discovered to enhance your ability for intimacy with self, with others, with God?

CHAPTER 9

SEXUAL INTEGRITY AND THE DIOCESAN PRIESTHOOD

BISHOP JOHN M. QUINN

In this chapter, Bishop John M. Quinn of Winona–Rochester, Minnesota, shares wisdom gained from experience in his service to the Church. As auxiliary bishop of Detroit, Michigan, he taught courses in theology at Sacred Heart Major Seminary and served as a spiritual director to many seminarians and priests. As bishop of Winona–Rochester, he served as an adjunct faculty member in the theology department of St. Mary's University of Minnesota in Winona. He has guided his priests and people through the difficult challenges of the sexual abuse crisis in the Church with the firm conviction that through this period of introspection and purification, we will emerge a stronger, Christ-centered, faith-filled people of God.

It is late Sunday afternoon. The Masses have all been said, the baptisms done, the family and parish events are over, and at about five o'clock the priest returns to the silence of the rectory. This is the experience of many persons, not just priests—to be alone and to be vulnerable in the quiet. What are their options? How are they to confront the silence in a healthy way?

The easiest option is to break the silence, to turn on the television or the music system and pour a glass of wine or some other drink. So far, so good, and it will probably lead to relaxation. All too often, however, this leads to a second glass of wine or the second or third drink that can trigger deadly temptations: becoming lost in unhealthy fantasies through adult films or pornography, indulging in self-pity over past disappointments or failures, nursing old resentments against rivals and perceived enemies. What then?

When I go grocery shopping, in the delicatessen section there are chickens roasting on a rotisserie for sale. The chickens turn over and over on the skewer until fully cooked. It occurred to me that all of us have a "rotisserie of the mind," with constantly revolving thoughts about broken relationships, hurtful moments, painful events and setbacks. These things continue to spin around in our thoughts, again and again, especially if triggered by alcohol and the fear of loneliness and silence.

The healthier choice is not to run from the silence but to move toward it as a natural part of being human. After one drink or glass of wine, put away the alcohol and call a friend or go outside for a walk and change the mood from self-introspection to some energy-driven activity. Or embrace the silence, seeing in those moments an invitation to be with the Lord, as a beloved son or daughter of the Father, and allow the presence of the Triune God to flood the heart with unconditional love and light.

Living in the Light: Priestly Celibacy and Self-Gift

Several years ago I was meditating upon the Crucifixion of the Lord in the Gospel of St. Matthew, and encountered the Triune God as one particular verse stood out and claimed my heart:

"They gave Jesus wine to drink mixed with gall. But when he had tasted it, he refused to drink" (Mt 27:34). Jesus refused the cheap wine that would dull his senses and reduce his pain and loneliness. In this gospel account, Jesus is an active and voluntary participant in the Father's plan for the salvation of the world. He doesn't take the cheap wine to make his suffering more bearable; instead, Jesus embraces the suffering with unconditional, sacrificial love that he gives freely to each of us.

That is the choice that priests often face after returning home exhausted from being fully engaged in priestly ministry, and from giving themselves generously in caring for their parishioners. Perhaps they are still stinging from an ill-placed comment by a critical parishioner, stated right before the beginning of the priest's third or fourth weekend Mass: "You never visit my mother in the nursing home. She gave money to build this church!"

Now, the truth of the matter might be very different. Perhaps the priest planned to visit or did visit, but the person in the hospital or nursing home has dementia and doesn't remember the priest's visit. Back in the rectory, after a few drinks, that incident is turned over and over on the mind's rotisserie, basting in self-pity. The evil one loves to see us wallow in anger and in self-pity, or to attempt to numb the pain with alcohol, drugs, pornography, fantasy, or anonymous sexual encounters. The holier and healthier choice is to move toward the light, to step back and ask God for the gift of humility so that you can learn from this encounter and let it go.

For example, the parishioner's comment may help you remember to call a family member after your next trip to the nursing home, letting them know you visited and saw their loved one. Turn off the rotisserie of self-pity in your mind and open your heart to the unconditional love of the Trinity. Follow close to Jesus, who did not take the cheap wine to get the strength to redeem the world. He embraced his unique identity as the beloved Son of the Father and was conscious of his identity to the end. Jesus poured out his love and forgiveness as he looked upon the crowd jeering and laughing at him as he redeemed the world.

As priests, we minister *in persona Christi,* sharing sacramentally in the one priesthood of Jesus Christ as beloved sons of the Father. The silence of the rectory and even the rejection of the faithful can be opportunities to turn to the Lord and ask to be filled with his loving presence. Human freedom transformed by the power of grace is directed toward clearing away the option of taking the cheap wine and instead drinking deeply from the very wellsprings that flow from the heart of Jesus Christ. For those of us called to the priesthood, our masculinity is expressed in celibate self-giving. For us, sexual and spiritual integrity is a lifelong process that requires living in the light of Christ in three important ways: in transparency, in accountability, and in surrender.

The Light of Transparency: Regaining the Trust of Our People

The Church is experiencing an intense period of introspection and purification due to the sins of clerics and prelates who betrayed the trust of God's people by sexually abusing vulnerable adults, young men and women, and children—or by covering up those crimes. It will take several generations and the healing power of grace to reclaim the credibility that was once enjoyed by the clergy.

As a young priest in my first pastoral assignment, I stopped at a large grocery store to pick up some snacks for an adult education program. I remember that it was raining, and the downpour never stopped. As I was leaving the store to run to my car in the rain, there was a mother who had a shopping cart loaded with groceries as well as a child in the cart and another in her arms. Even though she didn't know me, the mother saw that I was a priest and asked me, "Father, would you watch my baby while I go and get the car?"

I often wonder, *Would I be trusted by a new mother or father to watch their baby today?* Rebuilding trust takes time, but it can be reestablished. Having lived through the long period of sexual abuse scandals in the Church, I am convinced that grace is still abounding and that through this suffering, the whole Church is becoming holier and healthier as bishops, priests, deacons, and religious—along with the lay leadership—work together. Much reflection and healthy change has happened concerning the screening and formation of candidates in sexuality and celibacy, and teaching them to cultivate and sustain healthy friendships, not only among fellow priests but also with lay men and women. The seminary prepares a candidate for ordination, but God's people continue to form the priestly heart of the ordained.

Allow me to share a few examples from my life. At a parish assignment in my earlier years, I came to a deeper desire and love for the Eucharist because of fifty or more parishioners who attended the 6:30 a.m. Mass every day before going to work. Unlike me, they couldn't take a midmorning nap. In fact, many stayed for Bible study after Mass. I came also to appreciate the men and women who served on the parish council and the finance council, volunteered to be catechists, and engaged in Christian service. Without pay and often without dinner, they came straight from work and from family responsibilities to give me advice and to engage in planning parish programs and events because they loved Jesus Christ. Their sacrificial love radiated Jesus Christ and formed me into a better priest and servant. I am grateful for their friendship and patience with me.

Ongoing priestly formation involves commitment to the life-long integration of human and spiritual development and especially to sexual integration at every stage of priestly ministry. That commitment will allow grace to abound. None of this, however, will really be effective without a daily commitment to conversion and holiness. As one of my past spiritual directors once told me, "Give God a lot to work with, especially when the needs of the Church are great." In other words, be generous and let God use you as his instrument of reconciliation. Don't be stingy with God when laying down your life as an offering.

The Light of Accountability: Sexual Integrity, Masculinity, and the Priestly Life

Even after decades of celibacy, we must remain steadfast in constructively channeling our masculinity in thought, word, and deed—and in holding ourselves accountable through healthy relationships. Many years ago, before I turned sixty, I went shopping at a local grocery store. As I was standing in the produce section, a woman around my age came up to me and said, "You have nice legs." Since I was dressed casually and she had no idea that I was a priest, my response was an excited, "Do you really think so?"

When I checked out my groceries and returned to the rectory, I proudly told the other priest resident, "I still have it! I was told I have nice legs by a woman in the produce department." Not missing a beat, my brother priest asked me if the woman was carrying a white cane. My ego was punctured, and I was reminded that laughter assists with the serious work of integrating sexuality and spirituality through authentic interpersonal connections. These relationships take a variety of forms: in community with my brother priests, in healthy friendships with both men and women, and with a good spiritual director and other accountability partners within the work of ministry. These relationships need to be wholesome and free from the distortion of unequal power, the idolization of priesthood, and especially the use of another for personal satisfaction.

In my efforts to embrace the lifelong enterprise of sexual integration, I have found that boundaries are essential, especially as friends enter and leave our lives. Some friendships last over the years, while others are conditioned by place and time. What is important is knowing whether a friendship is helping to facilitate maturity and the integration of sexuality or is causing regression and a return to old ways that compromise living authentically as a priest.

In my work with seminarians, I often hear from those in formation that it can be difficult to maintain the prayer and devotional habits they acquired in seminary—the daily praying of the Liturgy of the Hours, Mass, and a holy hour—when home on long vacation periods. Meeting up with some of the old friends who filled their life before entering the seminary can cause a regression in their spiritual development because of the increased use of alcohol, crude language, or questionable media consumption, including pornography. As men preparing for priesthood, they may be challenged in their efforts to live in a way that allows them to sustain a daily prayer routine and maintain their public and private identity as a seminarian seeking sexual integrity, who upholds human dignity and respects the gift of human sexuality.

Isolation is not the answer. When the priestly life is devoid of healthy relationships, accountability diminishes and the pursuit of sexual integrity is all too often swept under the rug, causing natural masculine desires to resurface in unhealthy ways such as illicit and secretive "friendships" on one hand, or by evading real relationships on the other, becoming crusty bachelors with lots of material comforts. Neither of these coping strategies is conducive to a life of sexual integrity, or of a heart wholly converted to Christ.

Friendships that become unhealthy and do not facilitate growth in a life of conversion to Jesus Christ are best set aside, just as one sets aside clothes that no longer fit one's body or lifestyle. Over the years, I have tried to set boundaries and move toward spending more time with those persons who make me a better person. Because none of our friends are perfect (and certainly I am not perfect), we also need to be careful to set personal boundaries. Even with mature spiritual friends, I have found that observing certain boundaries is helpful in keeping my life in balance.

For example, I make it a point not to be out past ten or eleven o'clock in the evening. I belong back in the residence or rectory after ten. All of my married friends who treasure their spouses and remain accountable to them observe a similar protocol. After the meeting, the workout, or golf game, they call their wife on their cell phone and usually head home. After all, they have a spouse and children who need them, and they have jobs to go to in the morning that require early rising. They have taught me the value of boundaries that facilitate interior freedom to live out vocational commitments.

Overwork in priestly ministry is a common pitfall and an easy boundary to trespass, leading to a stressed and anxiety-driven life. I had to outgrow the belief that by working harder, I was becoming a better priest. The overwork squeezed out and reduced my time for prayer and leisure in an effort to accomplish more ministry. There was a clear danger of my becoming a mere functionary, whose efficiency and productivity in priestly ministry were beginning to erode and displace the personal, real, sacramental participation that was given to me when I was ordained into the one priesthood of Jesus Christ. While they are two sides of one coin, there is an important distinction between sacramental configuration to the one priesthood of Jesus Christ conferred at ordination, which is eternal, and the daily ministerial functions and tasks that flow out from the priesthood.

I have found that the best theology is done on my knees, in a position of humility and surrender to the Triune God. Over the past many years in which I have experienced the sexual abuse crisis, my prayer life has grown deeper, humbler, and more contrite. I pray especially for those who survived being victimized by priests and for God's faithful people, who in the midst of grave scandal continue to cling to Jesus Christ, present in the Eucharist, as they come to Mass every weekend. It is also a great challenge for me to pray for my brother priests who abused minors and the vulnerable.

As a bishop, I visit a different parish every weekend. After processing down the aisle, genuflecting, and kissing the altar, I turn to begin the opening rites of the Mass. As I look up, I am deeply moved to see God's people, present and faith filled, amid all the news reports and the media coverage about the way the Church handled the clergy scandals in the past. My faith is strengthened by the fidelity of God's people to the Eucharist and to the Church founded by Jesus Christ. If in the past I wasn't sure how to articulate and explain the theological concept of *sensus fidelium,* or "the true faith lived by God's people," it is very clear to me now. The Church is the work of the Triune God. Sin can deeply wound the members of the Church, but the Church will never be destroyed as the sacrament of salvation on earth for all the nations. Jesus never breaks a promise: "I am with you always, until the end of the age" (Mt 28:20).

Living as a man and as a priest with sexual and spiritual integrity is a lifelong process; it is never finished, even in the sunset years of retirement. It would be untrue to suggest that I have found the fail-proof way to integrate humanity with grace and to live my vocation to holiness and missionary discipleship without the least difficulty. Yet I have gained insights by listening carefully to those who live healthy, holy lives and by listening to the people to whom I minister, including survivors of sexual abuse. The people to whom we minister and those with whom we interact on a daily basis know whether our public and private lives give credible witness to our efforts to integrate sexuality into a life directed to the Triune God. When we fall short of this standard, we must return as often as necessary to the Source of the healing we seek.

In the Gospel of St. John (5:1–15), Jesus initiates a conversation with a paralyzed man who had been sitting for thirty-eight years beside the pool at Bethesda, waiting to be the first to get in after the angel stirred up the waters. He has remained there all these years, he explains to Jesus, because there is no one to put him in the pool. Jesus does not discuss or debate the validity of the excuses with the man who is paralyzed. Instead, Jesus asks one question, "Do you want to be well?" Immediately Jesus cures the man, who took up his mat and walked. So too, Jesus will heal our wounds; he does not want us to remain paralyzed by the current crises within the Church. Instead, Jesus invites us to stay on mission and bring the Gospel into our culture. We cannot do this until we have received the healing we need, so that we might live out that mission with integrity in our minds, our spirits, and our bodies.

Sexual integrity is the ongoing task of grace and human development at every stage of ordained ministry. It entails a lifelong commitment to respect the God-given sacredness and purpose of affections, desires, sexuality, and the dignity of every person in all relationships. It is the intentional living of a virtuous and moral life centered in Jesus Christ and his Church, sustained by the grace of the Holy Spirit.

"Do you want to be well?" is the question Jesus puts before each of us—his bishops, priests, and deacons as well as the laity. Wellness comes from knowing the true self with all its strengths and shortcomings, as manifest and transformed through grace, as a man ordained to the priesthood of Jesus Christ, endowed with interior freedom, who is called to integrate the gift of sexuality in ministry and in friendships, so that he seeks only the good of others. Christ's love is sacrificial and given freely. Sacrificial love is at the core of the priesthood of Jesus Christ, to which every priest is sacramentally configured at ordination. The Church has been deeply wounded by the sexual crisis; however, the Holy Spirit is renewing the priesthood of Jesus Christ by the call to holiness and wellness.

The Light of Surrender: Offering My Lifelong Yes

The lifelong journey centered in Jesus Christ and lived out in faith and service requires attention to sexual integration in a conscious and intentional manner. Sexual integration by a teenage boy who is fifteen is much different from the degree of integration of sexuality expected of a young man who is prepared to promise lifelong celibacy before ordination to the diaconate. At midlife, sexual integration takes a slightly different form as new questions emerge, along with fresh opportunities to surrender fully to God's call. At this time, for example, we must reaffirm that initial call in light of all the years of sacrifice with perhaps little or no public recognition. Was it all worth it? Having passed through those stages, am I deeply aware of the mercy of God and the support of my family and friends? Do I look with hope to living out with integrity and gratitude, to the end, the priesthood to which I was ordained?

Gratitude is the realization that everything and every blessing is a gift from God. Coming to accept that life is a freely given gift from God leads to a generous heart and a willingness to find opportunities to spend time with others, support worthy causes, and encourage and mentor the next generation. Generosity is at the heart of love and at the heart of the Triune God.

Bearing Witness to the Light

My favorite painting is *A Sunday Afternoon on the Island of La Grande Jatte,* by Georges Seurat. The first time I saw it at the Art Institute of Chicago, the 10 x 8–foot canvas was prominently displayed at the entrance of the gallery. The style of the painting is known as pointillism, as the artist created figures on the canvas using dots rather than brush strokes. This painting is best viewed at a distance; as the viewer comes closer, the figures disappear and become points of color on a large canvas.

I've often thought that the priestly life is a bit like that painting. If our lives are too closely examined and quantified, the reality of God's grace working on our humanity can disappear into separate points made up of our family history, notable successes, painful failures, and moments of guilt and shame, with no overall understanding of grace and God's plan. However, as we ask God for the gift of humility, and follow the call of the Triune God to communion and friendship, we begin to see, in the many dots that represent persons, events, and experiences in our lives, larger themes that reveal God's plan for our holiness and eternal salvation. Included in that plan is the integration of sexual desire into our Christian identity as beloved son and priest.

It is impossible to go to God without our entire humanity, including sexual desire, which God created as good. The power of God's grace can redeem and redirect all sexual urges and desires that have become distorted by original and personal sin, often manifest in a variety of disorders and addictions. Our entire humanity, including our sexuality, must be redeemed in the light of Christ. Without Jesus Christ, we are vulnerable to darkness and to sin. God's grace liberates and reorients human desire, so that it is purified and becomes the drive toward union with him.

One of the most important ways to live in the light, I've found, is to listen carefully to the concerns and insights of God's people, who rightly expect integrity from priests. My interactions with the lay faithful have been a constant source of fresh courage and truthfulness for me. Whether I am greeting them in the vestibule of a parish church after Mass, or listening to them at the meetings of the diocesan pastoral council, I appreciate the deeply held convictions and concerns the laity express to me as they reflect on their experience of the Church. For most, the Church is the place where they encounter the Lord and live out the mandate to preach the Gospel to build a community of faith and service, rooted in the Eucharist. Amid all the scandals, they love the Church and are willing to stay to fight to restore the integrity of the priesthood and to bring justice and healing to the survivors of clergy sexual abuse.

Over my years as a bishop, I have had to go to parish meetings to explain that I have removed a pastor because of sexual abuse accusations that are being investigated by law-enforcement officials. The hurt, anger, shock, and betrayal experienced by the parishioners is a cry from the heart that is overwhelming to hear. One time, at a parish that had its pastor removed, I brought with me seminarians to hear parishioners speak their words of pain at the open meetings, and I had the seminarians return with me at regular intervals to the parish for a holy hour of reparation. I wanted the seminarians to experience firsthand how a priest can destroy the faith of many people, but I also wanted them to see the resilience and tenacity of God's people to stay and help reform the Church they deeply love. I reminded them to be grateful for the *sensus fidelium,* the deep abiding faith of God's holy people, but not to be presumptuous or arrogant. To me, what I witnessed among those people was a powerful reminder that Jesus always keeps his promises to his Church. It is time for the Church, especially bishops and priests, to keep ours.

Sexual Integrity and Seminarian Formation

From my time spent with survivors of sexual abuse, reflecting on their experiences and concerns, I have come to see that we need to exercise even greater care and caution in the processes we use with seminarians, both in the discerning of their call to the priesthood and in their formation as whole and holy men of God. As a bishop, I am fully aware of the shortage of priests and the long journey to ordination, a process often lasting several years. And yet, we cannot lose sight of the goal of the formation process: a whole and holy man who can willingly and freely embrace celibacy, who has the maturity to surrender his natural, God-given desire for fatherhood in order to proclaim the kingdom of God, accepting the call to a generative spiritual fatherhood in the priesthood of Jesus Christ.

Wisdom dictates that this process cannot be rushed if we truly wish to regain the trust of the people of God. Yes, having fewer priests means more pastoral work for my brother priests, who are already stressed and overworked. However, there are no shortcuts to sexual integration. The power of grace interacting with human freedom, and the daily practice of virtue, takes time and cannot be rushed.

Sexual integrity flows from an interior freedom to live as Jesus Christ and to seek holiness by accepting boundaries in all relationships. For a priest, at the foundation of the interior freedom that is necessary for lifelong sexual integrity is the daily celebration of the Eucharist. It is in the Eucharist—in the liturgy and in our devotional lives—that we live out the sacrificial love of Jesus Christ in ministering to God's people. Among the necessary daily spiritual disciplines are a holy hour, praying and meditating on the sacred scriptures, and devotion to Mary. The external spiritual supports are not constraints but are to help facilitate interior freedom and living a virtuous life.

Priestly Celibacy Gift and Spiritual Direction

We have already examined a number of practices that are crucial to the well-integrated priestly life: nurturing healthy, long-standing friendships that are appropriately self-disclosive and accountable; and making time in a busy schedule for regular exercise, a hobby, and leisure. In addition, we all benefit from the regular reception of the Sacrament of Penance; some might also benefit from participating in a priest support group. And yet one thing more is needed: a spiritual director who is not a friend or golf partner.

When I have had to remove a priest from active ministry for the sexual abuse of a minor or a vulnerable adult, I find that *none of these priests are receiving direction from a spiritual director who holds him accountable.* Consequently, these priests wind up doing priestly functions without a priestly heart that is fixed in the heart of Jesus Christ.

A good spiritual director will help you to mature in your priestly calling. I once had a spiritual director who was blunt with me at the opening of every session. One session in particular has left an indelible impression on my memory, when he began with the question, "Are you ready to say goodbye to your youth?" I was taken aback by the question and didn't immediately respond. "Well, are you?" he challenged.

I thought, *I am forty-five, of course I'm still young, that's a stupid question to ask me.* When I didn't respond, my spiritual director said to me, "Not all the doors of endless possibilities are open to you anymore. You aren't twenty-five and you are too old to go to medical school or become an astronaut or an architect!" I realized he was asking me not merely about my youth, but about my willingness to embrace and surrender to God's providential plan at midlife, as I moved into the mature years of being a man and a priest.

While a youthful spirit is lifelong and comes from the joy of an intimate friendship with Jesus Christ, to cling to one's youth is to buy into a cultural construct that venerates youth and does everything possible to halt the passing of time. My spiritual director wasn't asking me to become old or set in my ways, but to let go of the false self to be loved unconditionally by the Triune God at a new stage in my life and to reaffirm a priestly life of sexual integrity.

When I finally realized what he was asking of me, I answered, "I am, but help me." Beginning with that session and after several sessions, I understood that the surrender of my youth to the Triune God was a reaffirmation of my saying yes to the initiative of God, who called me to priesthood and to a life of celibacy at age twenty-six. Now the question was presenting itself again:

Could I say yes again, as my hair was mostly gray, my body was changing, and multiple possibilities for different careers were no longer a real choice?

At the midpoint of life there is a choice to reaffirm the commitments made in the first half of life or to resist the natural consequences of those choices. Some try to turn back the clock in superficial ways, such as dressing inappropriately, dying their hair, or getting a toupee. Others express their fear in more serious ways, perhaps feeling anger toward those they perceive as having thwarted or derailed career plans, or resentment toward those who have not publicly recognized their talents and achievements. This can lead to an excessive use of alcohol, drugs, pornography, fantasy, and a loss of sexual integrity.

However, if we are willing to say yes to God's plan once more, the fear of growing old diminishes; death becomes a gateway to an eternal encounter with the Triune God. As we trust in divine providence and live out commitments begun in youthful years, we become reinvigorated in the second half of life—and become that much more beautiful to God.

My spiritual director was challenging me in his unique way. He wanted to know whether I was ready to reaffirm the free choice I made in the first semester of life, at ordination—with boundless energy and choices. Was I prepared to recommit myself in this, the second semester of life, as a beloved son of the Father, filled with the unconditional love of the Holy Spirit? As we continued to talk, I realized that this was in fact what I wanted: to live out my commitment to the self-giving priestly life of Jesus Christ as a generative, celibate witness to people in my ministry, and to live the meaning of sexual integration. To do anything that might diminish or damage that witness was an unthinkable alternative.

I was ready to affirm my commitment, regardless of the cost. I wanted to give myself entirely to God, just as my favorite saint and intercessor had done.

Fr. Damien of Molokai:
Priestly Intercessor and Model

Authenticity in the priesthood is measured by the desire to live a holy life rooted in the sacrificial priesthood of Jesus Christ, and to imitate the saints who have found the presence of Jesus Christ in the lives of the poor, the uneducated, the sick, migrants, sinners, and prisoners. Having a particular saint as an intercessor and role model opens doors to the integration of human development with spirituality and a life of compassion. My favorite saint is Fr. Damien de Veuster, better known as the leper priest, Damien of Molokai. He demonstrated for me the sacrificial love of Jesus Christ that a priest gives freely to his people.

When I was a very young priest, three of my priest classmates and I decided to go to Hawaii for a vacation. We economized by taking a package tour that included airfare and the hotel. Once we arrived in the airport on Oahu, the tour guides provided a warm welcome.

On the bus to the hotel there were about fifty people from around the USA. The bus driver gave a tour of downtown, along with a brief history of the Hawaiian people. Over the loudspeaker he called the tourists on the streets "missionaries." When asked why, he laughingly replied that many European missionaries came to convert the Hawaiian people, then built beautiful homes for themselves far removed from the people—all except Fr. Damien. He was a priest who lived and then died with those who had leprosy, as a leper on Molokai. The bus driver was proud to call Fr. Damien a true missionary. That remark kept coming up among the four of us. Was a hotel on the beach in Oahu the destination God wanted for us?

All four of us had gone to Catholic schools growing up and had heard our teachers extol Fr. Damien for his virtuous life. So upon arriving in the hotel room and after some frank discussion, one of my classmates placed a call to the rectory on the peninsula of Kalaupapa on Molokai to see if we could visit the place where Fr. Damien had lived, served, and died. The priest who answered the phone extended a warm welcome once he learned that we were priests. He also obtained permits for us to fly into Kalaupapa on a special flight. After meeting us at the landing strip, the priest, who was a member of the Congregation of the Sacred Hearts of Jesus and Mary, the same as Fr. Damien, took us immediately to the chapel where Fr. Damien celebrated Mass each day.

As we prepared for Mass, we noticed that there were no pews in the chapel. When we inquired about this, the priest encouraged us to look more closely at the floor of the chapel and to see small holes about two inches square at regular intervals. These spaces were used by the lepers, who could not sit up erect in a pew, and allowed them to pass their drool freely through the openings in the floor into the ground while attending Mass. It was clear that we were standing on holy ground. Without electricity or modern plumbing, and with minimal health care and medications, Fr. Damien had touched his people through the healing ministry and priesthood of Jesus Christ. Fr. Damien was their doctor, nurse, teacher, sheriff, counselor, and, most of all, their priest. He lived out the sacrificial love of Jesus Christ with his people.

After Mass, we were taken to the infirmary for a pastoral visit to those dying of Hansen's disease (leprosy). The priest told us to touch those whom we prayed with and to whom we offered the Eucharist. I knew, along with my classmates, that the priest's challenge to touch a person disfigured by a disease, who is lacking a nose, ears, fingers, or hands, or was severely disfigured, was really an invitation from the Lord. All of us learned a lesson about the healing touch of Jesus Christ as we blessed and touched the men and women with Hansen's disease from the United States and around the world. In turn, we received through them the healing touch of Jesus in our lives.

As we walked from the infirmary to his simple rectory, Father reminded us of the courageous witness of Sr. Marianne Cope, a Franciscan sister from New York who in 1883, at age thirty-five, came with six other sisters to assist Fr. Damien and provide nursing care for those brought to Kalaupapa. Sr. Marianne and Fr. Damien worked tirelessly to minister to the lepers and developed a deep friendship that was rooted in Jesus Christ and allowed each of them to live freely the witness of celibacy. Sr. Marianne loved the priesthood more than she loved Fr. Damien as a person, and Fr. Damien loved the consecrated life of Sr. Marianne more than he loved her personally. They observed boundaries in their relationship that allowed both to minister freely to a rejected population with love and service until the end of their earthly lives.

Once inside the rectory, the real question was posed to us. Would we be willing to stay for four days and be priest-chaplains while Father went to the mainland to take care of some urgent medical needs? It was clear what started out as a vacation to Hawaii had become a graced encounter and an invitation to meet the Lord in a fresh way. We all said yes, and we stayed until Father returned. We learned a valuable lesson—that brokenness and woundedness can lead to avoiding contact with those on the peripheries of life, but the Triune God will break through those barriers to summon the human heart into community and compassion.

In the many lonely nights and years that Fr. Damien experienced disease and suffering on Kalaupapa, what sustained his integrity, his authenticity? Although a member of a religious order of men, he was alone, and he knew that he could never leave Kalaupapa and go back to community life. It is apparent that Fr. Damien sustained his priesthood through the celebration of the Eucharist each day, along with a strong commitment to the Liturgy of the Hours and other devotions. Additionally, once a week, a galleon would dock at the Kalaupapa harbor and Fr. Damien would yell his sins up to a priest standing near the railing of the ship, who would grant him absolution. Humility most certainly must precede and accompany integrity, and will lead to a life centered in the Trinity that strives to keep human dignity at the heart of every relationship. St. Damien and St. Marianne, pray for us.

Conclusion

Just as dots of paint compose the image of a beautiful painting, or fragile threads interweave to form an exquisite tapestry, every person's life story is most beautiful when seen in the light of God's eternal plan. Whether the strands of our lives are bonded together and strong, or challenging and demanding like those of Fr. Damien and Sr. Marianne, by faith we can entrust ourselves to the Holy Spirit, who weaves together the fragile threads of our lives, with their joys and sorrows. Knowing that God's plan is infinitely greater than ours, we can persevere in faith and hope, our lives anchored in the definitive intervention of the Triune God manifest in Jesus Christ in human history. Each human life counts, and hope is so needed today.

Hope is a key factor in living out sexual integrity throughout all the seasons of life. Our entire bodies, our whole person—body, mind, and spirit—is redeemed by Jesus Christ and is destined for glory. In the Apostles' Creed we express hope for the "resurrection of the body," and in a future that is manifest in the Paschal Mystery celebrated in every Eucharist and made effective for every generation by the Holy Spirit.

We are made for union with God and for a future that is real and bodily, where we will be identifiable in heaven as men and women. Coming to see our life as part of the divine plan underscores the sacredness of the gift of human sexuality. How do I relate to others as a redeemed man in Jesus Christ who is preparing each day for entry into eternal life? Relationships matter in this world, because they will continue in the communion of saints in the world to come. Let us live in the real hope of a future that is founded in the Resurrection of Jesus Christ, the firstborn of the new creation.

Questions for Reflection

1. "Do you want to be well?" What have been the blocks or challenges you have had to work through as a priest in your quest for sexual integrity?

2. How has celibacy been a blessing in your relationships with fellow priests and parishioners in your ministry?

3. Has your commitment to daily prayer, celebration of the Eucharist, a daily holy hour, the Sacrament of Penance, and spiritual direction been a source of deepening your relationship with God and sustaining healthy relationships with others? If not, why not?

4. Who in your life has been a significant influence in addressing both the joys and challenges of integrating human sexuality?

CHAPTER 10

SEXUAL INTEGRITY IN THE FORMATION OF SEMINARIANS

DEACON JAMES KEATING

As a permanent deacon, husband, and father, and experienced formator of Catholic clergy, James Keating offers a unique perspective, having lived out the sacramental graces of both Matrimony and Holy Orders. In this chapter, Deacon Keating reflects deeply upon the question of what purpose is served by the celibate priesthood, and how both priests and married men are signs of a greater mystery: the purpose of every human to be united intimately with God alone.

The seminarian experiences the beauty of that call [to the celibate priesthood] in a moment of grace which could be defined as "falling in love." His soul is filled with amazement, which makes him ask in prayer: "Lord, why me?" But love knows no "why;" it is a free gift to which one responds with the gift of self. . . . [Seminary formation's] deepest goal is to bring the [seminarian] to an intimate knowledge of the God who has revealed his face in Jesus Christ.

—Pope Benedict XVI[1]

One of the first and most frequent questions anyone asks a seminarian is, "How are you going to live alone for your whole life?" This may be followed quickly by, "How are you going to live without sex?" Of course, these are the seminarian's questions as well.

In a culture where sexual activity is so often debased and abused through pornography and promiscuity, these questions reveal a profound misunderstanding about the nature of sex and its relationship to the spiritual life. Every aspect of human society has been deeply wounded as a result of this misunderstanding. Young adults are burdened by the pain and grief of hookup culture; families are destroyed through the normalizing of divorce and adultery; and lives are irreparably damaged from the failure of clerics to uphold their vows of celibacy.

No wonder, then, that the idea of "falling in love" in the way Benedict XVI describes has become foreign to many, or is considered too romantic, unrealistic, unattainable, too *ideal*. Of course, responding to beauty in an integrative and consistent way, ordered by self-gift, *is* romantic. Love by its very nature is romantic. Love is a choice *conditioned by being affected by beauty*, which elicits self-donation. The celibate is not one deprived of *pleasure*, but one who has been *captured by beauty*, the beauty of God. Such beguiling happens in the same way a young man is captured by the beauty of a woman and, from such an experience, discerns a call to make his body a gift to her.

Making a gift of one's body to another is the human response to falling in love. This gift is sacrificial, complete, and unconditional. The one who falls in love is the one who says, "I am not going anywhere. I will always be here to give my whole self, this body, to you." The object of a person's love, the one beheld as beautiful, responds to such attention out of the deepest part of the human heart, awakening the joy of being desired. Curiously, in Western society, love is often deeply colored with grief, sadness, and cynicism; it is defined in cautious, temporary, calculated, and self-protective ways. Society does not want to suffer, so it limits love to what can be controlled, denying the power of love to prevail over sin, over ignorance, and over time. And yet this denial cannot silence the deepest part of the human heart, which often unconsciously carries an ache to commune with God in prayer. Their grief notwithstanding, people want to love and be loved and, when awakened by beauty, are invited to *give*.

Because our reason and will are weakened by sin, we need to protect and order our choice to give *within* a lifestyle that nurtures, facilitates, and deepens our choice. In faith we call this lifestyle a *vocation*. The primary sacramental vocations in the Church establishing communion are matrimony and priesthood. Other forms of structured self-giving in the Church flow from baptism and vows (monasticism, secular institutes, consecrated life, hermitism, etc.). All of these vocations help sustain the choice to stay in love after we have fallen in love.

For the spouse and the priest, sacraments of vocation create environments of communion between the lover and beloved, ordering self-gift as one's regular life. Within married life, emotional and spiritual intimacy are the adhesives that hold spouses together in communion; similar intimacies bond the hearts of celibates to God. Born of self-revelation and donation, this communion becomes the very oxygen of the relationship. Intimacy in marriage is the mutual self-revelation of the spouses, generously sharing their intellect, affect, and bodies as gift. Any refusal to engage in self-revelation veils the original beauty that was seen and sought, and thus withers the capacity to give. The beauty of the beloved awakens desire for communion and reaches its fulfillment in sacrificial self-giving. The seed of beauty, planted when we fall in love, always blossoms upon the Cross, whether it be chaste celibate love or chaste spousal love.

The Priesthood Affirms the Good of Marriage

The experiences of couples falling in love are germane to chaste celibacy in priesthood because God does not call priests away from spousal love, but right into its white-hot center. It is good to remember that marital love is God's idea. It is a reflection of the way he fruitfully loves within himself. His own loves spill over in goodness as creation and redemption. God himself is self-giving to the persons within the Trinity; divine love overflows as life-giving gift, finding expression in God's ongoing creation and in Christ's spousal love upon the Cross.

In Christ, baptized disciples participate in this crucified and resurrected love, specified and particularized by way of the Sacrament of Marriage. But what of the celibate priest? Isn't his status a denial of the good of marriage? No. When lived authentically, celibate priesthood is marriage's greatest and deepest affirmation. Celibate priesthood blesses marriage, similarly to how God looked at creation and called it "good." When a man is seized by the beauty of God and falls in love with him, the priest's consequent celibacy and priestly life raises a question in married couples: "Can God be *that* real?"

The celibate's mysterious call is an object of contemplation for all married couples, for the celibate's prophetic life points to the ultimate love for which all humanity is destined: We were each made for God and God alone. Such a truth enables married couples to hold each other tightly, never demanding or searching for perfection in one another. The felt desire for perfection in one's spouse is simply a call to worship the one true God. Only he can satisfy that desire.

By adoring, loving, and worshiping God in his celibacy, the priest offers a true service to spouses. In noticing the priest's life, couples can say, "We too were made for God and not for each other alone." The celibate says to the married couple, "You see God in each other and know the consolation of his love in your mutual self-donation, but my sacrifice of marriage reveals the destiny of all. Ultimately, our souls rest only in God" (see Psalm 62).

Created to Rest in God Alone

Surprisingly, celibacy announces to our human nature that our spouse and children are *not enough* for the human heart. Our hearts were made for more. In grace, the celibate priest is called into the "more." He is invited to rest in God's consoling love alone. The celibate's deep prayer life both satisfies his own urgent longings[2] and gives witness to married couples that their deepest longings are also meant to be satisfied in God.

In both the celibate and marital expressions of human life, we know that we are created to rest in God. In prayer born of seeing the beauty of God as love, the celibate invites married couples to behold such love, first within the gift of their spouses. From the fruit of their love, they look beyond one another and together behold the eternal mystery of Christ in word and sacrament. Heaven is glimpsed through sacramental vocations and signs. All the baptized share concretely in the mystery of Christ's self-sacrificial love, known and sustained by the life-giving wedding feast that is the Eucharist.

If a seminarian wants assurance he is called to the priesthood, he must first be certain that he has fallen in love with the revelation of divine beauty. Priestly celibacy cannot be reduced to the practical; it has to be wholeheartedly romantic, or no man would ever embrace it for a lifetime in *his body*. In other words, priestly celibacy is both a sacrifice (of wife and children) and a consolation (deep contemplative prayer) in the body.[3]

The beauty of God in contemplative prayer must be regularly experienced as *consoling* if the priest is to be carried into and through *the sacrifice*. Such prayer cannot be just for monks, but must be found in all celibate vocations. Such prayer is in fact the very foundation of celibacy, whether lived in a monastery or in a suburban diocesan parish. Such intimacy with God is at the core of a total *formation in self-donation*. It makes up the heart of the relationships and disciplines we call the seminary. Celibate priesthood is not simply a way of life or a promise assisting us in avoiding mortal sin or a means to be more readily available to professional duties. It is a vocation to sacrifice the good of marriage and fatherhood by responding to a personal/ecclesial call to be taken up into Christ's own celibate, spousal love for the Church, his Bride.

Recognizing the Call to Priestly Celibacy

Priestly celibacy is a specific and personal call from Christ to sacrifice the good of marriage, the beauty of a woman, and the joy of fatherhood in order to espouse and father the spiritual needs of the Church, the Bride of Christ. It has to be this personal, this specific, if we are see it through to death. Without such specificity, chaste celibacy may be hijacked by human weakness, lived for lesser motives, or carried as an imposed burden.

This is where the vocation director plays a most vital role. There is much pressure to bring men into the seminary, leading to the temptation to define a man's suitability for priestly life according to natural personality traits. ("Father, I never really was interested in marriage.") Reducing the call to priestly celibacy to self-revelations of a natural personality fit is a temptation that ought not to be received so benignly. It is best to accompany such revelations from interested aspirants with caution. ("Why *weren't* you interested in marriage?" is the proper response from any vocation director.) The call to celibacy is not a cure for chronic loneliness or the last hope for a shy man. Nor is it the refuge for committed single men looking to seminary to give their chastity structure and discipline. Priestly celibacy is a "mystical identification" with Christ the Bridegroom.[4]

For the mature integration of chaste celibacy to be accomplished in a joyful way, the seminarian needs to know such a vocation did not originate within himself, but is a wholehearted response to a concrete encounter with the living God. Furthermore, it is a calling that is not his alone to discern; the Church discerns if this prayerful encounter was real. With this knowledge, the man is better able to weather the lonely times in seminary and the times of temptation or disappointment in ministerial life, and find a new level of peace during times of doubt or difficulty. "I didn't just dream up this call idiosyncratically. It was objectively confirmed by my formators and bishop." Celibacy is a personal call, but it may have its origins in a specific time of "falling in love" or in a more gradual apprehension of this loving call. Many seminarians report a personal moment wherein priestly celibacy was offered by God in prayer or in the midst of scripture reading or worship, as we can read in the testimonies below:

> When the call to priesthood came to me unexpectedly in prayer, it happened in a moment of incredibly deep encounter with the Lord and his personal love for me. It was a call to celibacy just as much as it was a call to the priesthood, insofar as I understood the call to be an invitation to belong to God alone. The whole movement of my heart was one of "falling in love" with God, and celibacy became so surprisingly attractive. Several years later, halfway through my seminary formation, I received a life-changing grace wherein I experienced Jesus Christ dwelling in me to such a degree that he filled me completely. That experience of communion came as confirmation of my vocation, and I could no longer imagine living for anyone but God alone.

And a second seminarian:

> It was near the middle of the Spiritual Exercises. I was around twenty-three and had fallen in love with Jesus about nine years before. I thought that he was calling me to the priesthood. I thought that he was calling me

to celibacy. I was asking for confirmation. Then, in the aloneness of silent days, I began to doubt. "This is hard. It feels lonely. Maybe I should pursue marriage instead." Relating this to God with honesty over the course of a few days, this desire for human intimacy only grew. But, through the relating, my real intimacy with God also grew. Then one day on retreat, I heard the Lord speak something like this into my heart: "You can leave. You can pursue marriage. I love you." Immediately, arising from the depth of intimacy into which God had been inviting me, I cried out in my heart, "No, Jesus, I want you." The desire for marriage never went away, but it was subsumed into a deep passion for spousal relationship with God—a spousal intimacy which fuels my day-to-day life, this life of celibate, spousal self-gift as a priest.

Other seminarians speak of a growing awareness that they are being invited to consider this kind of sacrificial life for the sake of the kingdom. Analogically we can speak of a man "falling in love" as if it was love at first sight or of a man who came to marry the "girl next door."

Becoming a priest is an idea that has been a part of my earliest serious memories. Even from an age as young as eight or nine. . . . Around puberty, I began to dismiss the idea of the priesthood as childish, and I did not seriously consider priesthood as a possible vocation during high school or at the start of my college career. In my sophomore year of college, as I got to know the new pastor at my home parish, I recognized just how shallow and empty my life had become. I felt as if I was living a lie and that the more I tried to run away from God, the harder he tugged back. And almost simultaneously to returning to the Church and beginning to pray, the idea, the desire, and ache for the priesthood began to resurface. I had to admit to myself that the desire and attraction for the priesthood had never actually gone away. I had taken it for granted and overlooked it. And yet this foundational desire had always been there. I cannot think of a specific moment I "knew" I was called to the priesthood. It was not so much an immediate experience of falling in love; it was a gradual recognition and acceptance that I was already in love. I did not fall in love with the priesthood like a flash of lightning. I just realized that, somehow, I had already fallen in love with it amidst the ordinary moments of life.

The first two men can pinpoint a time and a day of falling in love with God. This becomes a riveting story to be told and retold to willing listeners. The third man cannot pinpoint a time or place, because it appeared that God had always been with him, accompanying him through many changes, adventures, and—most importantly—ordinary hours of daily living. The personal encounter with Christ, in which he extends an invitation to join him in chaste celibate priesthood, can manifest itself in either of these ways. But a true invitation will last in fidelity only if the seminarian lives in the prayerful, personal, and living presence of the One who "was always there" or the One with whom he "fell in love" like a bolt of lightning.

The Goal of Seminarian Formation: Intimate Knowledge of God in Christ

We return to the quote from Benedict XVI with which we began this chapter: "[Seminarian formation's] deepest goal is to bring the [seminarian] to an intimate knowledge of the God who has revealed his face in Jesus Christ."

That initial encounter with Christ that the seminarian first experiences in prayer or over the course of his young faith life will develop into "intimate knowledge" within the seminary community. If the man has received a true call to sacrifice marriage and fatherhood in light of the overwhelming beauty of God's own love, then this initial gift of God will deepen within the formative relationships that constitute the seminary. The whole purpose of the seminary is to deepen the seminarian's interior life so he can internalize Christ the Good Shepherd's love for him as intimate knowledge and enter into communion with his pastoral charity.[5] This knowledge is not separate from academic study, but is larger and deeper than discursive knowledge alone. The seminarian who has truly encountered Christ lives within a more generous definition of study and knowledge born of his sustained engagement with the "face of Jesus Christ." He longs for a prayer-soaked study.

For the seminarian, integrating chastity within his body depends upon a work of grace and the acceptance of personal suffering. This grace-filled, prayerful suffering works in sync with a seminarian's self-knowledge and heals any immature self-centeredness. A priest is to be the very definition of mature love as he labors disinterestedly to secure the spiritual needs of his people. The priest's own spiritual and emotional needs are met in deep contemplative prayer, in substantive friendships with other clergy and laity, and within his sustained love of his own parents and brothers and sisters.

As a seminarian's prayer life grows, his certainty about the call to celibacy becomes clear and internalized. As he prays, the living God communicates this call to the seminarian in a definitive way, thus securing within the man a deep peace about sharing in the spousal identity of Christ the priest. As noted above, this very personal call is corroborated publicly by his formators through evidence of the seminarian's behavior and disposition. These two foci of discernment—the prayer-soaked conscience of the seminarian and the expertise of the formation staff—must be in sync. If the call is true, the man will be happy and the virtue of chastity will develop apace. If the call is not both personal and ratified within the ecclesial context (i.e., as a vocation, not simply an idiosyncratic desire), and the man remains in formation or even attains priesthood, inevitable "sadness" will occur with all the attending compensations in behavior. Integrity is sustained by a real appropriation of an authentic call to priestly celibacy and the judgment of the formators in the seminary itself, turning aside pressure from those who may not know the seminarian as well. Seminaries must be places of free discernment: the staff ought not to be cheerleaders for any one vocation, encouraging a man to "stick it out" or "keep trying."

Sexual Integrity in Seminary

The greatest enemy to a seminarian's sexual integrity is the presence of fear within himself or seminary culture. Seminary is a time that allows Christ to come alongside a man, deepen his discipleship, configure him in a mystical way to Christ's own priesthood, and support him in developing an "undivided heart."[6] It is not a time for a man to accept a divided heart as his normal interior state.

True relationships of discernment, established by the diocesan vocation office, should be set up before seminary begins, to explore whether a man has received an authentic call to chaste celibacy. The simpler set of relationships, either informally established between a man and his vocation director, or more formally rooted within a house of discernment, should focus only on *deepening prayer* and *clarifying priestly celibacy as a vocation*. Seminaries do feel pressured to keep enrollment up, satisfy bishops who need future priests, and calm seminarians' anxiety (and perhaps distraction) as they strive for academic and pastoral formation success. If the celibacy issue could be answered prior to seminary (perhaps college seminary can help here, but I am thinking of a simpler accompaniment by the vocation office where there is no institutional expectation to have the man "advance" in any way), the weight of this momentous decision would be lifted and the man could participate more freely in his formation.

Of course, discernment by the Church regarding evidence of priestly fitness in competencies, personality, and virtue remains in play. Whether a man discerns celibacy before entering the seminary or during formation, it is vital to *bring the seminarian into intimate knowledge of God by contemplating the face of Christ*. This way of discerning is not arcane, but simple and effective. In the end the man will come to a conclusion about the way God is calling him to become a saint. This way in itself is not the way of the Cross; it is a way of consolation and joy.

God doesn't call men to be sad. He calls them to his side so that they can espouse either a woman in Christ or the mission of the Church in Christ. Being with Christ in the proper vocation produces great consolation and joy that sustains a man in fidelity when the Cross appears. And the Cross *will* appear whenever love invites self-renunciation. Our vocation is not a cross; crosses come within our vocations as love bids us to die to self.

How to Acquire Intimate Knowledge of God

To live in intimate knowledge of God by contemplating the face of Christ is to become vulnerable through deep prayer to the mysteries of Christ's own life. This prayer is scripture based, eucharistically engaged, and expressed publicly as ministry. This prayer (along with human formation, psychological counseling, the study of philosophy and theology, and good mature friendships) assists the seminarian to internalize the truth about himself in the light of Truth itself, Christ. This formation readies him to sacrifice one form of spousal love (marriage) and take up another form as "he lays down his life for the sheep."

All husbands, either as priest or as spouse, *lay down their lives*. In the words of John Paul II in his letter to priests:

> The priest, who welcomes the call to ministry, is in a position to make this a loving choice, as a result of which the Church and souls become his *first interest*, and with this concrete spirituality he becomes capable of loving the universal Church and that part of it entrusted to him with a deep love of a husband for his wife. The gift of self has no limits, marked as it is by the same apostolic and missionary zeal of Christ, the good shepherd.[7]

This articulation by John Paul II defines the spousal imagination: the woman or the Church becomes a man's "first interest." Because of this disposition, a seminarian's self-donative commitment yields life and produces fruit. This can only happen, however, if a man has first received love and been capable of receiving love; otherwise, he may use others in his quest to be known, to be loved.

One doesn't enter priestly formation to find love. Those who have already known the love of God seek formation as a response, so that this love might grow into compassion for those who have not yet known God's love. Benedict XVI expressed this clearly:

> Anyone who wishes to give love must also receive love as a gift. Certainly, as the Lord tells us, one can become a source from which rivers of living water flow (cf. Jn 7:37–38). Yet to become such a source, one must constantly drink anew from the original source, which is Jesus Christ, from whose pierced heart flows the love of God (cf Jn 19:34).[8]

The truth expressed here by Benedict XVI is an articulation of the very origin of celibacy and an expression of how we can be sustained in such a vocation.

Conclusion: What Are Integrated Seminarians?

What, then, are integrated seminarians? We return one more time to the words of St. John Paul II: "The Church and souls become his first interest."[9] A seminarian or priest can only have the Church as his first interest if he is fundamentally fascinated with God, if he "constantly drinks anew from the original source, which is Jesus Christ." Mysticism moors ministry. By mysticism, I mean the penetration of the mysteries of Christ into a person through prayer and sacramental worship. Unless the celibate cleric is securely fascinated with God, ministry can become a *search for communion* rather than the fruit of living communion with God.

The mission of the seminary system is to form integrated men possessing a holy, affective maturation. They suffer this maturation within their own bodies as they develop psychological and affective health, a deep rich prayer life, charitable service to those in need, and conversion through an understanding of and a love for doctrinal and theological truth. This integration happens in the messy, sometimes annoying, and always grace-filled environment of peers, formation mentors, spiritual directors, and teachers. These seminary relationships should also expand to include more women, laypeople, permanent deacons, and families.[10] Sexual integration is completed in seminary by the suffering of a deeper reception of divine love in prayer, yielding a new heart that wants to serve, not to be served (see Matthew 20:28).

Seminaries must build a very strong gate into priestly formation. The Church is not desperate for priests; she is desperate for holy, mature priests who think of the needs of others because their own affective needs are being met in sacramental and personal prayer, familial relations, and sound peer friendships. A man ought not to become a priest if he simply "wants to help people." A man becomes a priest because he wants to yield his whole body to God, and in the service of pastoral charity, through a life of celibate love.

A priest's desire to "help people" flows from having received divine love at a level that satisfies his need for love. Seminaries need to accept men who are established in love by family, capable of entering holy friendships, sustained in deep prayer, and desirous of spending their lives in pastoral charity. Seminaries must nurture relationships within which God is sought, encountered, suffered, and loved, during which a man will come to want God *in* the priesthood. A vocation will be revealed to formators as a seminarian reveals his true heart as he suffers within the four areas of priestly formation: human, spiritual, intellectual, and pastoral formation.

Bishops ought not to retain inadequate candidates out of fear there will be few priests. Instead, they should concentrate on finding seminarians who are vulnerable to being formed into men like this:

Seminary formation offered me a grace-filled time of contemplation and meditation on the gift of the priesthood and God's call to celibacy as a way of spousal living. My most profound awareness of this was shortly after my pastoral internship, while in prayer before the Blessed Sacrament, when I identified my deepest need, not coming from my ego or from the comfort that any other person could provide, but from communion in Jesus Christ. In that moment I felt my whole identity found its purpose, joy, and fulfillment in the self-gift of priesthood.

Questions for Reflection

1. Do you recall the moment or events that confirmed that Christ was calling you to share in his own chaste celibate life?

2. How does being called to celibacy affect the mode, depth, and content of your prayer?

3. What is the gift celibacy brings to ministry?

CONCLUSION

PATRICIA COONEY HATHAWAY

In my introduction, I suggested that what is missing in contemporary books on a Christian approach to sexuality is the personal witness and testimony of men and women who have struggled to understand and live by the Church's teaching on sexuality and, in so doing, model for us what the integration of sexuality within our spiritual lives looks like. And so, I invited men and women from every walk of life to share their personal stories and professional insights on this most sensitive and complicated topic. They took up the challenge, and in the process addressed some of the most crucial questions regarding the relationship between our sexuality and our spiritual lives that we face today:

Why is there so much confusion about the role of sexuality in our lives?

Why has sexuality been reduced to having what is often meaningless sex, demeaning the personhood of both parties?

What are the origins of the addictions that plague our culture and our world?

Why is the tremendous power of sexuality experienced by so many (and so often) not as a force for love, life, and blessing, but as a source of hurt, pain, confusion, and disappointment?

In sharing their stories, our contributors have borne eloquent witness to the idea that attitudes toward sexuality can either hinder or facilitate our growth in a healthy spiritual life. In reflecting on his appreciation of John Paul II's theology of the body, Fr. John Riccardo pointed out that when he was young, he heard from various teachers over and over again, "Don't do that. Don't do that! Don't even think about doing that!" But nobody ever told him what *to* do. Finally, he notes, he was getting some answers and they made sense.

All of our authors, including Fr. Riccardo, have offered answers regarding how they perceive the relationship between human sexuality and the spiritual life. Their insights, which have come out of their lived experience, provide fresh perspectives as to how to live out our sexuality within a vibrant, mature Christian spirituality.

The task before us is a daunting one because most Catholics are not accustomed to talking openly about sexuality; nor are many comfortable having a conversation about what they consider the private world of their personal spirituality. Put those two areas together, and what normally follows is silence. To help end that silence, this book includes questions for reflection and discussion at the conclusion of each chapter. These questions are meant to spark much-needed conversations about the connection between human sexuality and the spiritual life between people from a variety of backgrounds and states of life—singles, young adults, seminarians, deacons, priests, religious, friends, and married couples. It is highly likely that some of the most fruitful conversations will take place among those who are walking very *different* paths, in order to come to a better understanding of how the Holy Spirit calls each of us to a particular state of life precisely because the one, holy, catholic, and apostolic Body of Christ *needs* this diversity in order to accomplish our mission here on earth.

Principles of Sexual and Spiritual Integrity

I'd like to summarize a few of the essential principles that have emerged from the wealth of insights shared by our authors.

First Principle: Love as Our Purpose

As pointed out by St. John Paul II, we cannot live without love. We remain incomprehensible to ourselves; our lives are senseless if love is not revealed to us. Our search for love, our yearning to love and be loved, is fulfilled within the intrinsic connection between our human sexuality and our spiritual lives.

In her chapter, Sr. Sara Fairbanks expressed the meaning of this connection: "Sexuality is a complex concept that most basically refers to our love energy, the yearning for intimacy and connection that emerges in our lives even before we are born."

Consequently, we are in need of a spirituality that recognizes a core truth: that the very energy that moves us toward communion with one another is the same energy that moves us into a relationship with God. From this perspective we can say that sexuality and spirituality are two sides of the same coin. Both express a deep longing to know and be known, to love and be loved, by God and others.

Second Principle: The Meaning of Personhood

In her chapter, Janet E. Smith reminds us that Pope John Paul II grounds our sexuality in the notion of what it means to be a person capable of knowing, loving, and choosing the good; that is, the capacity to transform self-centeredness (the sexual urge to use someone for our own pleasure) into true love (seeking only the good of the other). We saw this principle at work in every author's description of their journey toward sexual integrity.

As an example, Timothy O'Malley described the crucial role of parents as the first teachers of human sexuality. It is within the family that the child first discovers what it means to be a human being—often through the mundaneness of daily life. O'Malley provides us with much food for conversation around how to help parents be more intentional about instilling in their children healthy attitudes toward their sexuality and its expression at every stage of development.

Third Principle: The Journey of Conversion

The conversion of mind and heart was a priority in Jesus' proclamation of the Gospel. Mark's gospel begins with Jesus' words, "This is the time of fulfillment. The kingdom of God is at hand. Repent, and believe in the gospel" (1:14–15). All our authors spoke about the necessity of ongoing conversion in their lives.

The Greek word *metanoia* refers to a radical turning or redirection; a turning *away* from those dehumanizing patterns of thought, values, and actions that keep us from becoming the women and men God intends us to be. In his chapter, Daniel Keating emphasized that the path to mature sexual integrity involves a deep conversion of mind and heart. Intellectual conversion, while necessary, isn't enough. We also need conversion of the will, which involves the quest for authenticity between one's private and public selves. That quest necessitates a turning away from pornography, sexual fantasies, alcohol, drugs, masturbation, and other disordered ways of dealing with loneliness, stress, and the anxieties of life and ministry.

Conversion also involves the turning *toward* and living out of those thoughts, values, and actions that enable us to become the women and men God intends us to be. Timothy and Karen Hogan described four paths of conversion: (1) From shame to gratitude; (2) From self-focused to relation focused; (3) From knowing everything about the other to embracing and exploring the ongoing mystery of the sacred other; (4) From legalism to authentic discernment. While the Hogans applied these four paths to married life, we can explore their implications for other states of life as well.

Fourth Principle: A Recovery of the Virtue of Chastity

As we noted above, all people are called to deep conversion, and that includes chastity in mind and body. The *Catechism of the Catholic Church* describes chastity as "the successful integration of sexuality within the person and thus the inner unity of man in his bodily and spiritual being" (2337). In his chapter, Daniel Keating includes a quotation from St. John Paul II regarding chastity within a celibate commitment, that can be meaningfully applied to men and women in every state of life: "In virginity and celibacy, chastity retains its original meaning, that is, of human sexuality lived as a genuine sign of and precious service to the love of communion and gift of self to others" (*PDV*, 29).

Expanding on this notion, the pope goes on to say that formation in sexuality for the celibate [and for anyone] "should be truly and fully personal and therefore should present chastity in a manner that shows appreciation and love for it as a virtue that develops a person's authentic maturity and makes him or her capable of respecting and fostering the 'nuptial meaning of the body'" (*PDV*, 44).

A commitment to chastity is a hard sell in today's world. It is out of step with an overly sexualized culture where many young adults and adults view sex as no big deal and express fears of intimacy and commitment. Many authors today use the term "sexual integrity" to express the meaning and intent of the virtue of chastity. Is this a helpful solution?

Fifth Principle: The Gifts of Spiritual Friendships

All of our authors expressed the conviction that close, healthy friendships are essential for nourishing and sustaining sexual integrity. I thought of the advice given by the great mystic St. Teresa of Avila to her sisters regarding the need for good friends, that is, the ones who will be honest with you. In *The Way of Perfection*, she writes:

> Love such persons as much as you like. There can be very few of them. When you begin to strive after perfection, you will at once be told that you have no need to know such persons—that it is enough to have God. But to get to know God's friends is a very good way of "having" God, as I have discovered by experience, it is most helpful. For, after our Lord, I owe it to such persons that I am not in Hell.[1]

In her chapter, Susan Muto distinguishes the characteristics of true friendships from those of pseudo-friendships. True friendships, she states, begin in Christ, continue in Christ, and are perfected in Christ. Christ stands between soul friends so they never focus exclusively on one another. Among spiritual friends, prudence directs; justice rules; fortitude guards; and temperance moderates. Pseudo-friendships, on the other hand, are often undertaken without deliberation, are indulged in imprudently, are oblivious of how they affect others, and are governed more by passion than reason.

True friendships must be tested to be sure Christ is at the center; yet they greatly aid us in overcoming self-centeredness, pride, and envy. In her chapter, Eve Tushnet reminds us that learning to love well in and with our bodies is complicated for everyone. Because our contemporary culture sexualizes physical affection between adults, it can be especially hard for laypeople living celibately to receive warmth and comfort. She admits that "it can be both frightening and humbling to ask for the touch we need. And yet it is so worthwhile because of the beauty and peace we experience when we find trustworthy friends who won't take advantage of us, with whom we can relax—as John lay trustingly against his Lord, our truest Friend." Surely much of the loneliness, sense of isolation, and depression people of all ages experience today could be avoided if we knew how to cultivate, sustain, and nourish healthy, wholesome, nonsexualized friendships. Learning to love well with our bodies is an important area of honest discussion among those in every walk of life.

Best Practices of Sexual and Spiritual Integrity

Below are just a few of the best practices our authors recommended for cultivating a healthy, wholesome sexuality within the context of a mature Christian spirituality. None of these recommendations are new; in fact, they have been tried and proven true throughout the Christian tradition. Our authors reflect on them through the lens of nourishing and sustaining a life of sexual integrity.

Prayer

The gospels remind us that Jesus drew his strength and power from spending time with his Father in prayer. As disciples of Jesus, we are invited to do the same. All of our authors spoke about the necessity of encountering Christ through prayer as the means of growing in our relationship with him and receiving the grace to live a life of sexual integrity and spiritual maturity.

In his chapter on the formation of seminarians, Deacon James Keating states that a celibate is not one deprived of *pleasure*, but one who has been captured by *the beauty of God*. Such a discovery, he acknowledges, only happens through prayer, which he describes as an intimacy with God that is at the core of a seminarian's total formation in self-donation. Fr. Riccardo shared that more than thirty years ago someone encouraged him to start the day with a holy hour before the Lord, and it is the single best habit he knows.

He describes well the fruit of such prayer: "If I am honest with God there, really bring him the brokenness, unveil the wounds, and listen for his voice and receive his love, then I depart from his presence better able to bring that same love and consolation to the many people I will meet that same day." Similarly, Jeff Jay identified the necessity of cultivating a relationship with God (as we understand him) if we want to be healed of the compulsions and addictions that sap our freedom, hold us hostage, and destroy our lives. Our authors remind us, then, that "there is need of only one thing" (Lk 10:42): giving prayer a central place in our lives, resisting the world around us that debunks the need for an interior life and a relationship with God. This is a challenging area of discussion for all of us today.

Spiritual Direction

I was struck by Bishop John M. Quinn's observation that he has yet to remove a priest from active ministry for sexual abuse who had been receiving spiritual direction from a director who would hold him accountable.

There are many forms of spiritual direction available. Spiritual *guidance* refers to assistance in spiritual development received through homilies; casual conversations with a priest, deacon, or an ecclesial lay minister; or spiritual formation opportunities such as scripture study courses, adult education programs, and programs like Alpha or Encounter. The ministry of spiritual *direction* refers to a more formal process by which a trained spiritual director and directee meet regularly (often once a month) to help the individual grow in their relationship with God and to discern how God is working in their life. Its overall goal is to help individuals recognize God's presence in every dimension of life. To be effective, spiritual direction requires an openness to guidance on the part of the directee, a willingness to be vulnerable and transparent even about sexual struggles and those areas of concern that may block the individual's growth in union with God and in genuine love of others.

Discernment of Spirits

The practice of discernment of spirits finds its origin in the personal experience and teaching of St. Ignatius of Loyola. It refers to the art of listening to our inner selves and learning how to recognize those thoughts and feelings (Ignatius referred to them as "movements") that arise from the Holy Spirit and our true selves, as opposed to those thoughts and feelings that arise from the evil one (whom Ignatius identified as the enemy of human nature) and our false selves.

In his own life, Ignatius endured a period of convalescence as a soldier by reading the only two books available to him: one on the life of Christ, and the other on the lives of the saints. As he pondered the life of Christ and the deeds of St. Francis and St. Dominic, Ignatius discovered that he desired to emulate them and noted that these thoughts and desires brought him a peace and consolation that remained with him long after his reading and reflection. On the contrary, when he imagined the honors he would receive at the royal court in the service of a certain lady and the armed exploits he would perform in her service, he gradually recognized that these thoughts initially gave him pleasure but later left him feeling dry and dissatisfied.

When Ignatius became aware of the contrasting spiritual experiences, his teaching on discernment of spirits was born. In his teaching, Ignatius assumes that God communicates directly with us through our thoughts, feelings, and desires; but he also recognizes that the evil one communicates with us as well. Thus, we need to learn how to recognize those thoughts and feelings that come from God and the true self and follow them, whereas we should resist and turn away from those that come from the evil one and our false selves. Daniel Keating describes the importance of going through a disciplined process of discernment over a lengthy period to determine the genuineness of a call—in his particular state in life, to consecrated celibacy. Yet discernment should not be reserved only for the big vocational decisions of our lives. It should become a way of life. As one priest observes:

> Years ago I learned how to discern spirits in critical matters, but it is only in recent times that I have learned to live at such a depth of ongoing self-awareness that I discern rather continually and habitually. It is also significant that many small but important discernments have to do with what TV programs I watch or what books I read. More and more the Lord is showing me what to avoid and what to enjoy, and how these entertainment inputs are immensely powerful in their effects on me and my apostolate.

The Examen of Consciousness

As a way to practice discernment of spirits, Ignatius developed what he calls the examen of consciousness. Its purpose is to help us become intentionally present to God as each day unfolds: *Where do I recognize God's presence and respond accordingly? Where did I not recognize him or resist his invitations?* Ignatius recommended that all Jesuits and anyone else who wants to deepen their relationship with God make the examen once or twice a day—ideally around noon and in the evening. He recommends that this prayer be kept short—ten or fifteen minutes maximum—otherwise, the pray-er will not persevere in it.

The prayer of examen consists of five steps:

1. Gratitude: Thank God for the gifts and blessings of the day.
2. Petition: Ask the Holy Spirit to lead you through a review of the day.

3. Review: With the Holy Spirit as guide, look back over the day. Identify those thoughts, feelings, and actions that were of God and brought peace, joy, and a sense of alignment with his will; and identify those that were not of God that brought restlessness, sadness, or feelings of being out of sync with his desires for us.

4. Repentance: Ask forgiveness for any mistakes or failures.

5. Renewal: Resolve, in concrete steps, to live tomorrow well.

Timothy and Karen Hogan spoke of practicing the prayer of examen in order to cultivate a heart of gratitude. This practice helps them to celebrate where God is working in their lives and guides them as they pray for each other's successes, challenges, and difficulties. The examen is a well-established way of keeping us honest and intentional in attending to our human and spiritual growth.

Participation in the Sacramental Life of the Church

Our authors describe two sacraments as essential for growing in our relationship with God and sustaining a life of sexual integrity: the Eucharist and Reconciliation (or Penance). The Hogans noted that the movement from a place of shame and struggle to a place of grace and gratitude came in the midst of celebrating the Eucharist. Jeff Jay concluded his chapter with the question Jesus asked of the crippled man by the pool at Bethesda: "Do you want to get well?" (Jn 5:6). Bishop Quinn reminds us that this is a question Jesus puts before all of us—to which all of us would say yes!

The Sacrament of Reconciliation, through which we encounter Jesus' healing touch, has fallen out of use for many Catholics. Some no longer feel the need for a community of worship within which to express their love of God or to seek reconciliation with God and others. Yet, unless we participate in a community of memory that celebrates who we are and what the purpose of our lives is, we live at a superficial level, without an anchor or guide to the fullness of life. Surely a retrieval of the importance of the sacramental life of the Church is one of the most crucial challenges facing us in this period of purification and renewal. All of these authors have witnessed through their lives that the challenges and graces of the hard-fought battle toward integrity, wholeness, and intimacy is worth the effort, for it leads to the emergence of the true self in self-giving love and service of God and others. So, let us move forward, ever mindful of the words of Jesus: "I have come so that you may have life and have it to the full" (Jn 10:10).

NOTES

Foreword

1. In a 2006 essay, Alice von Hildebrand said that friendship is a "remnant of paradise." She quotes St. Augustine, who recalls the loss of a childhood friend, observing, "O madness which does not know how to love men as men should be loved" (*Confessions*). Hildebrand's essay appeared in *Crisis*, "The Canons of Friendship," https://www.crisismagazine.com/2006/the-canons-of-friendship. See also Paul Senz, "Holy friendship is 'a remnant of paradise,'" CatholicPhilly.com, April 13, 2018. St. Aelred said, "He who abides in friendship abides in God."

2. After Fr. Donovan's funeral, Fr. James Martin wrote this in *America*: "As the coffin of my friend left the church, I turned back and, through tears, saw a space entirely filled with David's friends. And, more than ever before, I saw the value of being a good priest who does a few simple things very, very well. He prays. He listens. He loves. And most of all, he takes delight in God's people" ("Of Many Things," *America*, January 30, 2006, https://www.americamagazine.org/issue/558/many-things/many-things).

3. Josef Pieper, *The Four Cardinal Virtues* (Notre Dame, IN: Notre Dame Press, 1966), 205.

Introduction

1. Erikson, as quoted in Don S. Browning, *Generative Man: Psychoanalytic Perspectives* (New York: Dell Publishing, 1975), 21.

2. Janet K. Ruffing, R.S.M., *Spiritual Direction: Beyond the Beginnings* (Mahwah, NJ: Paulist Press, 2000), 60.

3. Christopher West, *Theology of the Body Explained: A Commentary on John Paul II's "Gospel of the Body"* (Boston, MA: Pauline Books and Media, 2003), 10.

4. Ronald Rolheiser, *The Holy Longing: The Search for a Christian Spirituality* (New York: Image, 2009), 31.

5. Rolheiser, *Holy Longing*, 193.

6. James B. Nelson, *Embodiment: An Approach to Sexuality and Christian Theology* (Minneapolis, MN: Fortress Press, 1978), 105.

7. James B. Nelson, *The Intimate Connection: Male Sexuality, Masculine Spirituality* (Louisville, KY: Westminster John Knox Press, 1988), 28.

8. Benedict XVI, *Deus Caritas Est* (2005), Vatican website, http://
www.vatican.va/content/benedict-xvi/en/encyclicals/documents/
hf_ben-xvi_enc_20051225_deus-caritas-est.html.

1. What Is Sexual Integrity?

1. Aristotle, *Nicomachaen Ethics*, trans. Hippocrates G. Apostle (Des
Moines, IA: Peripatetic Press, 1984).

2. Karol Wojtyła, *Love and Responsibility*, trans. Grzegorz Ignatik (Boston, MA: Pauline Books and Media, 2013).

3. Wojtyła, *Love and Responsibility*, 17.

4. Wojtyła, *Love and Responsibility*, 105.

5. While *Love and Responsibility* is essentially a philosophical text, it
occasionally dips into scripture for indispensable principles. The "norm"
that we are to love others finds its most solid basis in revelation—in the
scriptural teaching that we are to love others as ourselves.

6. Wojtyła, *Love and Responsibility*, 27.

7. Wojtyła, *Love and Responsibility*, 214.

8. Wojtyła, *Love and Responsibility*, 154.

9. Wojtyła, *Love and Responsibility*, 155.

10. Wojtyła, *Love and Responsibility*, 122.

3. Sexual Integrity and the Challenge of Addiction

1. Interview with Kenneth M. Adams, PhD, and Jeff Jay, Royal Oak,
Michigan, February 19, 2019. *Note*: In one recent study of people twenty
to thirty-five years of age, 95 percent of males and 52 percent of females
had looked at pornography in the last six months. In addition, sexting
(the transmission of intimate personal images via text or apps) has
become commonplace.

2. Interview with Kenneth M. Adams, February 19, 2019.

3. Telephone interview with Deborah Schiller, MSC, LPC, CSAT and
Jeff Jay, February 27, 2019.

4. *Definition of Addiction*, American Society of Addiction Medicine,
adopted April 12, 2011. Note: the ASAM definition was updated after the
writing of this chapter. However, the definition is still accurate for our
purposes. https://asam.org.

5. Deborah Schiller interview, February 27, 2019.

6. Deborah Schiller interview, February 27, 2019.

7. Deborah Schiller interview, February 27, 2019.

8. The help of clergy, particularly through the Sacrament of Reconciliation, can also be extremely helpful in addressing spiritual issues. But
talking with people who are suffering from the same problem as we are is

often easier and less embarrassing than talking with the parish priest, at least initially.

4. The Joyful Dance of Sexual Connection

1. Dr. Hendrix, a former Protestant pastor, is the creator of Imago Relationship Therapy. We were given a copy of his first book, *Getting the Love You Want*, for a wedding present. This book helped us to embrace marriage as a sacramental vocation that prompted us to transformation and sanctification.

2. John Paul II, *Familiaris Consortio*, 16, emphasis ours.

3. *Editor's note:* Prior to Pope John Paul II, the Church was largely silent on the issue of whether a married person could both enjoy an active sex life and pursue personal holiness. The Church has not formally acknowledged, for example, whether married saints such as Thomas More were sexually active. More recently, Thérèse of Lisieux's parents were canonized, and obviously they were sexually active; in addition, John Paul II tried to explicitly address this issue. And yet, as the Hogans point out, the Beltrame Quattrocchis did choose to forgo sexual intercourse.

4. Ronald Rolheiser, *The Holy Longing: The Search for a Christian Spirituality* (New York: Random House, 2014), 193. We found Chapter 9, "A Spirituality of Sexuality," to be thoroughly life-changing.

5. Some scholars see personalism as the theme that most distinctively and consistently runs through St. John Paul II's writing. For a summary, see Avery Dulles, "John Paul II and the Mystery of the Human Person," *America*, February 2, 2004.

6. Vatican Council II, *Gaudium et Spes*, 16.

5. Sexuality, Spirituality, and the Single Life

1. John Paul II, *Familiaris Consortio*, 11.

2. *Holy Mass on Boston Common: Homily of His Holiness John Paul II*, October 1, 1979, 5, Vatican website, http://www.vatican.va/content/john-paul-ii/en/homilies/1979/documents/hf_jp-ii_hom_19791001_usa-boston.html.

7. Growing in Sexual Integrity as a Consecrated Man

1. One of the characteristic marks of many of the new ecclesial movements is the renewal of the charism of celibacy, both for men and women. In nearly every instance, the groupings of celibate men and women experience the call to be joined with families in one larger community, where the two vocations can complement and support one another. To learn more about the Servants of the Word, go to servantsoftheword.org.

2. Yves Raguin, *Celibacy for Our Times*, trans. Mary Humbert Kennedy (St. Meinrad, IN: Abbey Press, 1974), 69.

3. John Paul II, *Pastores Dabo Vobis* (1992), sec. 29, Vatican website, http://w2.vatican.va/content/john-paul-ii/en/apost_exhortations/documents/hf_jp-ii_exh_25031992_pastores-dabo-vobis.html.

4. Thomas Dubay, *". . . And You Are Christ's": The Charism of Virginity and the Celibate Life* (San Francisco: Ignatius Press, 1987), 81.

5. Raniero Cantalamessa, *Virginity: A Positive Approach to Celibacy for the Sake of the Kingdom of Heaven* (New York: Society of St. Paul, 1995), 65–66.

6. To make clear, I am speaking here about contexts above and beyond the confessional, which has its own specific grace and order.

7. Cantalamessa, *Virginity*, 42.

8. Issues of sexual abuse should be handled properly according to protocols for sharing and reporting about potential sexual abuse, past and present.

9. Cantalamessa, *Virginity*, 74, 75, emphasis in original.

10. Adolphe Tanquerey, *The Spiritual Life: A Treatise on Ascetical and Mystical Theology*, trans. Herman Branderis, 2nd rev. ed. (Rockford, IL: Tan Books, 2000), 518.

11. Tanquerey, *The Spiritual Life*, 521.

12. Dubay, *". . . And You Are Christ's,"* 57.

8. Love and Intimacy as a Religious Sister

1. Fran Ferder and John Heagle, *Tender Fires: The Spiritual Promise of Sexuality* (New York: Crossroad Publishing Co., 2002), 233–34.

2. Ferder and Heagle, *Tender Fires*, 29.

3. Ferder and Heagle, *Tender Fires*, 27.

4. Catherine of Siena, *Set Aside Every Fear* (Notre Dame, IN: Ave Maria Press, 2020), 103.

5. L. J. Milone, *Nothing but God: The Everyday Mysticism of Meister Eckhart* (Eugene, OR: Resource Publications/Wipf and Stock, 2019), 111.

6. Teresa of Avila, *The Interior Castle*, trans. Kieran Kavanaugh (Mahwah, NJ: Paulist Press, 1979), 35.

7. From *Finding God in All Things: A Marquette Prayer Book* (Milwaukee, WI: Marquette University Press, 2005).

8. William A. Barry and William J. Connolly, *The Practice of Spiritual Direction* (New York: Seabury Press, 1982), 68.

9. David Richo, *How to Be an Adult: A Handbook on Psychological and Spiritual Integration* (New York: Paulist Press, 1991), 12.

10. Richo, *How to Be an Adult*, 20.

11. Richo, *How to Be an Adult*, 18.

10. Sexual Integrity in the Formation of Seminarians

1. Apostolic Journey to Cologne on the Occasion of the XX World Youth Day: Meeting with Seminarians: Address of His Holiness Pope Benedict XVI, August 19, 2005, Vatican website, http://www.vatican.va/content/benedict-xvi/en/speeches/2005/august/documents/hf_ben-xvi_spe_20050819_seminarians.html.

2. John Paul II said it best in referencing how a chaste celibate draws from the source of love for his own consolation when he commented upon St. Joseph's chaste life with Mary: "Joseph, in obedience to the Spirit, found in the Spirit the source of love, the conjugal love which he experienced as a man. And this love proved to be greater than this 'just man' could ever have expected within the limits of his human heart" (*Redemptoris Custos* [*On the Person and Mission of St. Joseph in the Life of Christ and of the Church*], 1989, sec. 19, emphasis mine).

3. By contemplative prayer I mean that communication between a man and God within which he beholds the beauty of Christ's own mysteries: his life, ministry, death, and resurrection. This beholding is secured by a real love for God, one that is secured affectively by the honest self-revelation of the man in response to the honest and full self-revelation of the Son of Man. This beholding and self-revelation is the bonding adhesive of spiritual intimacy.

4. Jorge Carlos Patrón Wong, "Foundations of Priestly Formation," Congregation for the Clergy website, http://www.clerus.va/content/clerus/en/notizie/new4.html, accessed November 4, 2018.

5. Congregation for the Clergy, The Gift of the Priestly Vocation: Ratio *Fundamentalis Institutionis Sacerdotalis* (December 8, 2016), secs. 41–43, 89.

6. Congregation for the Clergy, The Gift of the Priestly Vocation, sec. 110.

7. John Paul II, *Pastores Dabo Vobis*, sec. 23, emphasis mine.

8. Benedict XVI, *Deus Caritas Est* (2005), sec. 7.

9. John Paul II, *Pastores Dabo Vobis*, sec. 23.

10. Congregation for the Clergy, The Gift of the Priestly Vocation, secs. 13, 95ff., 119, 120, 125, 137, 150–51, 205.

Conclusion

1. Teresa of Avila, *The Way of Perfection: The Collected Works of Teresa of Avila*, Vol. 2. (Washington, DC: ICS Publications, 2012), 6.

Patricia Cooney Hathaway is a professor of spirituality and systematic theology and the chairperson of the licentiate in sacred theology degree committee at Sacred Heart Major Seminary, where she has worked since 1987. She is the author of the award-winning book *Weaving Faith and Experience*. She also serves as the associate editor of *Human Development Magazine*.

Cooney Hathaway earned a doctorate of philosophy specializing in systemic theology, spirituality, and human and spiritual development from Catholic University of America, where she also received a master of arts degree in religious studies. She has a bachelor of arts degree in English from Marygrove College and also earned a certificate of spiritual direction from the Consortium of Theological Colleges and Universities. Cooney Hathaway is a member of the Catholic Theological Society of America and Spiritual Directors International. She is also the recipient of the Life Directions Founders' Lifetime Achievement Award and The Splendor of Truth Award from the Catholic Lawyers Guild. Her work has appeared in publications including *Mosaic, Human Development Magazine, Seminary Journal*, and *America*. Cooney Hathaway speaks throughout the United States and Canada.

She lives with her family in Detroit, Michigan.
www.shms.edu

Rev. John Riccardo is executive director of Acts XXIX and the host of *Christ is the Answer* on EWTN radio. He is a priest of the Archdiocese of Detroit.

AVE

AVE MARIA PRESS

Founded in 1865, Ave Maria Press,
a ministry of the Congregation of
Holy Cross, is a Catholic publishing
company that serves the spiritual and
formative needs of the Church and its
schools, institutions, and ministers;
Christian individuals and families; and
others seeking spiritual nourishment.

For a complete listing of titles from

Ave Maria Press

Sorin Books

Forest of Peace

Christian Classics

visit www.avemariapress.com

AVE MARIA PRESS
Notre Dame, IN
A Ministry of the United States Province of Holy Cross